C000089665

CRIMINAL
WIRRAL II

DANIEL K. LONGMAN

The History Press

For Ryan Leeke

With special thanks to

Roger Phillips

Mark Minshall

Peter Almond

Tom Belmar

First published 2009

The History Press
The Mill, Brimscombe Port
Stroud, Gloucestershire, GL5 2QG
www.thehistorypress.co.uk

© Daniel K. Longman, 2009

The right of Daniel K. Longman to be identified as the Author
of this work has been asserted in accordance with the
Copyrights, Designs and Patents Act 1988.

All rights reserved. No part of this book may be reprinted
or reproduced or utilised in any form or by any electronic,
mechanical or other means, now known or hereafter invented,
including photocopying and recording, or in any information
storage or retrieval system, without the permission in writing
from the Publishers.

British Library Cataloguing in Publication Data.
A catalogue record for this book is available from the British Library.

ISBN 978 0 7524 5007 0

Typesetting and origination by The History Press.
Printed in Great Britain

CONTENTS

FOREWORD

As a phone-in presenter on BBC Radio Merseyside it always amazes me that so many people ring in after suffering at the hands of some criminal or other and conclude by saying that such things never happened 'in their day.' There were no cases of child abuse, no cries of rape, no murders, no criminal gangs (apart from the Krays), never an incident of burglary or theft and everybody could leave their house unlocked without a second thought. And on the Wirral? Well, the Vikings might have been here centuries before committing their wild acts of rape and pillaging, but in the more recent past it was quite a genteel and refined sort of place; nothing like it is now with all sorts of anti-social behaviour and the like.

Yet this book puts paid to all those myths. Dan Longman has collected together a wide range of newspaper cuttings from the past and retold them so that they really do come alive. And he's created some great chapter titles, with 'What the Butler Did' and 'The Prenton Lane Maniac' as two of my personal favourites, but what really makes this collection so fascinating is the way Dan has literally taken the bare bones of each story and then used his skills of research, his thorough knowledge of the period and his imaginative abilities to allow the reader to 'live' through each tale. These true stories of crime on the Wirral help to create a genuine picture of the peninsula in days gone by and it's the sheer variety of the stories that is so interesting. From the retired seaman robbed and imprisoned in his home by masked intruders (just the sort of crime you'd expect to watch recreated nowadays on the BBC's *Crimewatch*) to the newly married couple whose row led to a potential murder charge against the groom. Then there are those stories which are just plain weird, such as the RSPCA investigation into the cruel slaughter of pigs, or the way a father personally investigated alleged impropriety by his daughter's piano teacher.

All in all, this book makes you realise that nothing changes. Virtually all of the events could have taken place in this century, in this day and age. Human beings are still equally cruel, stupid, jealous, vindictive and criminal, but thank goodness such people are, and were, a minority.

Truly all of human life is in here and Dan relates it all with such wonderfully graphic detail. It's definitely the kind of book to put by your bedside and treat yourself to each evening before drifting off to sleep (but to dreams or nightmares I dare not say!).

Roger Phillips
BBC Radio Merseyside

INTRODUCTION

The Wirral is becoming somewhat notorious for a shocking spate of murders, killings and general criminality. In the past few years our little peninsula has been host to a fair few examples of such acts which have managed to achieve local and national infamy.

On 29 March 2007 at approximately 2 a.m. David Currie, a transvestite, arrived at Steven Boyd's home in Stanley Avenue, Wallasey. He had made the hour-long trip from Manchester to engage in some 'private business' with Mr Boyd, who had been drinking and taking drugs. Just before 3.30 a.m., Mr Boyd texted a mutual friend on his mobile phone to say Mr Currie, known as Angela, had fallen unconscious, but it was a further thirty minutes before he called for an ambulance. It was soon discovered that Mr Currie had sustained serious internal injuries during the rampant sex session and had suffered a heart attack. Paramedics managed to resuscitate the man, but he died later in hospital. Before Judge Gerald Clifton, Steven Boyd denied unlawful killing but confessed to drinking and taking cannabis and cocaine. His defence was that his dog, Tosh, a great dane-bull mastiff cross was somehow to blame for the death. The story didn't wash and Boyd was sentenced to five years for manslaughter.

On 9 August 2007, elderly market stall holder Bashir Ahmed was attacked at his flat in The Woodlands by thirty-one-year-old Gerard Murphy. He had heard a rumour that the trader was in the habit of keeping his takings at home. Murphy and a fifteen-year-old accomplice broke into his property but were spotted by Mr Ahmed and a struggle broke out. Bashir was afterwards found lying in a pool of his own blood by concerned work colleagues. A subsequent medical report showed severe bruising, six loosened teeth and a complete fracture and dislocation of the spine. The sixty-three-year-old was left paralysed from the neck down, his life ruined and with injuries compared to those of a high-velocity traffic accident. Judge Clifton at Liverpool Crown Court sentenced Murphy to a minimum of eleven years in prison. The sidekick youth was given only a six-month detention and training order.

Bonfire night saw a further atrocity take place on our borough's streets as care home runaway Jamie Smith (son of the aforementioned Gerard Murphy) committed a despicable murder. The child who was only thirteen years of age had been boozing on cider and vodka on grassland near to the YMCA on Whetstone Lane. It was the misfortune of local man Stephen Croft to fall into the hands of the youth and suffer a succession of unprovoked kickings and beatings until dead. Mr Croft had turned to alcohol after an industrial accident some years previously and on the night of his death was five times over the legal limit, totally senseless. That night his battered body was thrown onto the very bonfire he had been drunkenly watching and left to burn.

On later examination a pathologist found, as well as substantial charring, severe bruising over the right eyelid, the nose to be very swollen with the nasal septum and the right side of the nasal bone both fractured. Blood gushed out from the nose and mouth during the course of the procedure. For this display of total disregard for human life, Jamie Smith was sentenced to serve thirteen years in prison.

These cases are just a small selection of the recent unsavoury goings on in our part of the world. But despite my subtle pessimism, I believe the claim that the Wirral has 'become notorious' to be slightly inaccurate. It is in fact no different to any other region. The whole country seems to be on the decline as the front pages have turned into nothing more than carousels of criminal newsprint. It horrifies me – and I'm sure you – to read reports that prisoners have been released mid-sentence due to overcrowding. As a Special Constable, I believe the most obvious answer is surely to build more prisons. Releasing the nation's prisoners early is not the answer.

In 1901 the average prison population was 15,900. At the time of writing, inmate figures stand at approximately 83,000. From this you would be forgiven for believing that the good old days were relatively crime-free, but I can assure you things were not *sans souci*. Even now, after a good few years of researching, I am still surprised by some of the stories that pop up in the pages of the *Liverpool Mercury* and *Birkenhead Advertiser*. Britain has a fantastically varied and fascinating history of crime and Merseyside in particular has witnessed some of the most shocking, cruel and perplexing examples of such. I predict crime writers of the future shall have rich pickings in researching our little county and dissecting the long-forgotten reports of the *Wirral Globe*, scouring hours of footage of Gordon Burns at Northwest Tonight and searching through vast numbers of intriguing internet sites to discover the hard facts about our modern-day contemporary atrocities.

This book, the third in the series, hopes to entertain and inform. It has been impossible for me to paint a picturesque view of the past, as it never existed, despite what the elder generation may claim. Again I have attempted to include a varied selection of criminality, ranging from the horribly horrific to the candidly amusing, but above all I hope you find the choice of tales interesting.

Read on and uncover the grisly facts of what once lay floating in Birkenhead Park pond, a gruesome suicide on board a Woodside-bound locomotive and the farcical actions of a drunken butler one night at the stately Thurstaston Hall.

Daniel K. Longman, 2009

LOOSE LIPS SINK SHIPS

One night in the year 1890 the then popular seaside resort of New Brighton was malformed into a lurid stage for a murder that stunned the nation. The town was renowned far and wide for its bright and breezy atmosphere, but it was thrust into the public spotlight when a grisly crime created a more macabre mood.

Felix Spicer was a retired mariner. At sixty years of age he should have been happily settling down and enjoying his later years, but this was not to his character. On the contrary he felt as young as ever and even had a two-year-old son. Little Tom Spicer was an adorable wee lad who idolised his older siblings: Felix, William, Gertrude, Annie, Ethel and Harry. Their mother, Mary, was originally from Wales and a youthful thirty-one years of age. She ran a small café at 3 Birkley Parade in Victoria Road, catering for the thousands of tourists and amusement-seekers the town was famous for. To the outside world the Spicers seemed a perfectly happy family; adorable children, a comfortable home and a loving marriage. But things were not as rosy as they seemed.

The Monday after Easter week saw Mary take the day off to ride the ferry to Liverpool, leaving her husband in charge of the café. He was quite competent in managing it and had done so on numerous occasions without any problems. On closing up at the end of the day, Felix put the day's takings safe upon a shelf in the kitchen, happy with a hard days work. Mary returned to the café later that evening and put the money deep into her dress pocket.

'Leave that money there!' Spicer snapped.

'It does not take two to take the money,' she snapped back. A clash of raised voices saw Mary prevail as she asserted her rightful authority. 'You have no business here. I am mistress.'

There had been frequent bouts of bickering regarding her husband's place in the business ever since his return from sea the previous September. Felix wished to include his name above the door and be manager but Mary objected. The quarrel persisted until Mary's patience finally snapped and she refused to

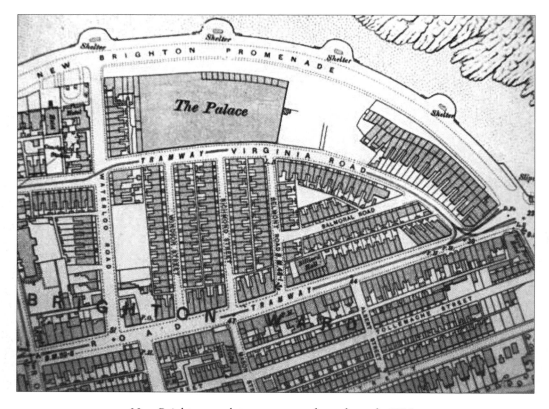

New Brighton, as shown on a map from the early 1900s.

go back with Felix to their home at 18 Richmond Street, saying that she had had enough of him and was going to sleep instead at the café.

'Fine!' Felix shouted, and stormed off home in a huff. He was a terribly stubborn man, much to his own occasional detriment. The argument played on the old man's mind all night and he just couldn't let the issue lie.

The following morning Felix made his way round to the café to have some more stern words with his wife. How dare she speak to him like that? He had a sly card up his sleeve. The old mariner strolled into the shop with a proud swagger and beckoned Mary over with a wrinkled hand.

'You told me last night I had no business here. I will show you who is master!' The seaman cleared his throat. 'My name is Felix Spicer, but there is no such name as Mary Spicer!'

Mary was mortified. The landlord, Mr Wright, was in full earshot and was more than a little surprised to hear Felix's claim. It became startlingly clear to all present that after all their years together the Spicer's had never actually married. Mary's cheeks burned bright red with a dangerous mix of

Victoria Road, the location of Mary's café, as seen in 1902.

embarrassment and pure hatred. It wasn't long before a policeman had to be called to the scene and separate the feuding pair as Mary went berserk. On the sergeant's advice Felix left the café to calm down and give Mary some space to compose herself. The old mariner expected his wife to return home and make up in a matter of hours, but he couldn't have been more wrong. She was adamant in her refusal to go home and quite content to stay at the café, well out of the way of the man whom she had now come to detest. Her own customers were gossiping in hushed tones, but anything was better than living with the horrible man who had caused her so much embarrassment.

Felix was equally keen not to lose face. That was, however, until the following Saturday, when his stubbornness finally subdued. He popped a letter into the refreshment rooms asking Miss Palin, as Mary was now known, whether he would be allowed to work at the café again for Whit week. It was really just a ploy to get back into her good books in a far-fetched hope to rekindle their sham marriage. The reply stated in no uncertain terms that Mary did not want him working there, not on Whit week or any other week.

She never wanted to see him again. As far as she was concerned he was out of her life for good and his warm-hearted plan had failed. However, this was just a minor setback and Spicer supposed that a personal visit would make the woman see sense. At half-past nine that night Felix put on his coat and knocked on the door to the café. He was met with the unloving sound of a bolt fastening and a softly spoken yet strict reply of, 'I can't. I'm undressing.'

'Open the door Mary, please.'

'Go home Felix, just leave me alone. Good night!'

Felix begged her to let him in so that they could talk but she wouldn't budge. The old man was forced to return home alone to Richmond Street, feeling miserably rejected and alone. He chatted with his son, William, and a lodger by the name of Alfred Short, whilst trying his best to appear cheerful, but his mind was preoccupied. It was getting late and Spicer put the children to bed. 'Good night,' he said lovingly, before giving each one a kiss on the forehead. He gently closed the bedroom doors and left the youngsters to drift peacefully off to sleep.

At about midnight, a lodger and waitress at the café, Ann Fraser, arrived home from work. She had witnessed first-hand the terrible effects the breakdown of the relationship had been having upon the couple and it was she who often had to tolerate both party's stressful mood swings. Mrs Fraser noticed Felix and nursemaid Maria Fearon having heated words in the kitchen and thought it best to keep out of the way. 'Good night,' Ann waved coyly as she began heading up to her room. 'Night,' replied Mr Spicer gruffly. 'I'm going to sit up for a lodger and sleep on the sofa.' Ann thought he seemed irritable, but that was the norm nowadays and she paid no real attention to it. The argument between the bad-tempered householder and his staff steadily escalated and the noise of the confrontation woke up Mr Short, who had been trying to sleep upstairs. Maria was sent to bed as Felix's nerves could no longer cope with the aggravation. He was an old man who was already suffering from some serious stress and he genuinely feared a heart attack or some sort of breakdown to be just around the corner.

As the night drew on the house began to settle down and its varied members fell into deep sleeps. The lodgers, children and nursemaid were all out like a light. Felix Spicer, however, was not. The hours ticked by and with every minute Mr Spicer's mind became more and more disjointed. Who would want a retired sixty-year-old with the burden of young children? How could Mary be so callous? If he couldn't win her back then there was nothing worth living for.

These thoughts danced about forebodingly in his brain. By three o'clock in the morning Felix had worked himself into such a state that he had lost all sense of normality and rational thought. He acquired a knife, six inches long and razor sharp, and headed up the stairs. With a gentle turn of the handle he pushed open the door into William and Harry's bedroom and edged in. Snug in their beds their father saw them sleeping softly, top to tail on the single mattress. The fourteen-year-old's neck was soon in contact with the wooden-handled blade as it sliced through William's windpipe. The shock caused the lad to bolt upright from his peaceful slumber. Blood splattered out in a semicircle across the bed sheets, surging forth from a stalk of severed veins. As he struggled, his gargled cries awoke his younger brother. Within a minute the toddler too was dead; blood dripping from similar wounds across his tender throat. In another room eight-year-old Gertrude had been disturbed by the commotion. 'What's the matter?' she called out with a yawn.

'Nothing. Go to sleep and shut up,' Spicer hissed, and he made his way downstairs and out of the house.

Over in the refreshment rooms Mary Palin was oblivious to the very recent loss of two of her children as she slept alone in her improvised bed. It was about half-past three when the silence of the dark, lonely streets of New Brighton were broken by hard hammering upon the door and the sudden smash of window glass. Mary awoke with a fright and jumped out of bed in her nightclothes. A bearded Felix was trying to break in downstairs and she saw him reach through the broken window pane with a bloodstained arm, desperately feeling the lock for a key. There was no key, so Felix punched in a second pane and attempted to climb through it. Fear swam through Mary's whole body. Her unhinged ex was after her and she had to escape fast. The woman's survival instincts took over and she fled towards the first broken window, away from Felix, and began climbing out onto the parade. Her reflexes however were not fast enough and, despite his age, Spicer was able to make a grab at Mary, pulling her down onto the pavement. 'Murder! Murder!' she screeched as her body thumped against the concrete.

'You scream murder but you won't scream murder in a minute you bloody wretch, when I am done with you!' Felix was holding a brandy-soaked handkerchief and fought to smother it over Mary's mouth. She was able to swipe it from Spicer's grasp and began screaming and shouting even louder than before. Through watery eyes she saw something glimmering in his breast pocket. A pistol she thought, but it was in fact a knife; the very same knife used to kill William and Harry. He pulled it from his pocket and attempted to stab his terrified victim, but Mary was proving to be a more than worthy match and was able to deflect each and every strike aimed at her exposed throat. 'For God's sake please Felix! For the children!' she cried. But Felix had gone too far to stop now. Mary was forced to grab hold of the blade itself, causing blood to slide down the cold metal like a crimson serpent. She pulled up her skirt to cover her neck in the hope of some defence whilst continuing to tighten a painful hold around the knife edge. The scuffle sent the weapon flying free of Felix's hand and Mary saw her chance to escape. She ran past John Bailey's grocers in a petrified panic and over towards a cab man's hut. Spicer was in pursuit and a deadly game of cat and mouse commenced around the small taxi building.

'Oi!' Mr Bailey had come down to his doorway and demanded to know what Mr Spicer was playing at. Felix was in a long overcoat, a peaked cheese-cutter cap and a pair of bloodied splinter-laden slippers, and brandishing a blade. The shopkeeper was met with an outburst of foul insults as Felix remained fixated on catching his prey, a petrified Mary Palin.

'Mary! Mary! Come quick!' Bailey beckoned, and without a second thought the woman raced into the shop in hysterics. Blood and tears ran down her face as she stood shaking behind her saviour. Mr Bailey bolted the door and stared in disgust as Felix Spicer calmly made his way back down the parade.

Neighbours contacted the authorities and PCs Potts and Jones, along with the proprietor of the local Bon Marche store, Francis Storey, were soon knocking on the door to 18 Richmond Street.

'We want you Mr Spicer,' said one of the officers, and the elderly man found himself being led away to New Brighton police station for some stringent questioning.

'I have done nothing wrong,' said Spicer, though his attire suggested different; with bloodstains on the wrists of his shirt, his trousers and a large patch on his right knee, he looked well and truly guilty. A scanty excuse of mere red paint did not wash with the lawmen.

At half-past four his interview began and it soon became ominously obvious that a search of the house at Richmond Street was urgently required. Sergeant Cooper and Constable Potts returned to the property and conducted an investigation. PC Potts headed upstairs and knocked on the door to Alfred Short's room. He explained to the lodger what had happened and asked to be shown to the boys' bedroom. Alfred obliged without question and showed the officer where the two lads were sleeping. Of course the children were not sleeping, but lying dead amongst reddened bed sheets. The police were dealing with a double murder.

Following an inquest Felix Spicer was sent to stand trial at Wallasey Police Court before a trio of magistrates headed by Captain Molyneux. Charged with two counts of murder and attempted murder the mood of the court was

The property in New Brighton where Felix Spicer committed the atrocities.

one of complete and total revulsion. He was attired in a simple brown jersey with a plain white neckerchief and listened to the evidence against him with great attention.

His surviving victim, the somewhat traumatised Mary, took the stand and revealed the rocky history that was her 'marriage'.

When I was sixteen he took me away from my home in Cardiff and promised to marry me when he got back from sea, he being about to take a voyage. He took apartments for me, and placed me there until he returned. When he came home from sea he received a letter from a friend, Mr Kershaw from New Brighton, requesting him to go there and he sent for me in a fortnight's time on a promise that he would marry me then.

The woman wept quietly through the course of her evidence, occasionally wiping away a renegade tear from her check.

> Felix sent me to Birkenhead for a license sometime after this and kept putting me off from time to time. He was fearfully violent; I was always in terror of him. I left Felix several times but he always followed me and brought me back, and threatened that if I did not submit to his will he would kill me.

A letter was read to the court. It was penned by Miss Palin shortly before her attempted murder and was a clear written reprimand to the man who had attempted to woo her favour in a letter of his own:

> Mr Spicer, this in answer to your daring to ask me to make up. You must be mad to think I shall ever speak to you again, much less make it up. You told Mr Wright I was not your wife. You mean, contemptible scrawl! Did you think of my tears? When Felix was born I begged you to marry me out of my shame and you laughed at me! But I have waited and the day has come. I can tell everyone my tale. Don't think it was for liking of you that I waited. I hated you since the day you laughed at me. I'll go to the gallows before another night under the same roof as you!

Mary was asked to give her view on Felix's relationship with the children, particularly William and Harry. Just why did he choose to murder his own sons?

'My husband was on the best of terms with the children and was very affectionate to them. He never struck them at all.'

'When you use the word husband you mean Mr Spicer?'

'Yes sir,' Mary replied shamefully.

Evidence was given by Dr Bircle, who told the court that he believed the boys to have been dead for about three hours by the time PC Potts found their bodies. The cutting of the throats was undoubtedly the cause of death.

Interesting testimony came from the nursemaid, Maria Fearon. She stated that the mysterious lodger Felix had been waiting up for actually arrived at the house before she went to bed. Miss Fearon said that her master had in fact told the man that there was no room in the house and that he would have to turn him away. After being handed his umbrella the man left without any trouble.

The weapon, a six-inch blade with a dark wooden handle, had been brought back by Spicer from a December voyage aboard the *Claremont*. It was heard how he had commented that it was worth half a crown and would apparently settle all in New Brighton if needs be. It was certainly a dangerous instrument capable of the most appalling physical injury. Mary Palin knew that all to well. She sported a nasty cut to her nose and her hands were still suffering from her grappling the blade with bare palms.

The magistrates consulted and ordered their prisoner to face a higher judge at the Chester Assizes. It was there on 31 July that Felix's fate was determined for all eternity.

Spicer's lawyer, Mr Wood, fought strongly on behalf of his client. He argued that the blood on Felix's clothes might reasonably be accounted for by the smashing of the window at the café, not the killing of the children. On the contrary, Felix loved all his children dearly. It was the defence's view that the mysterious lodger, of whom very little was known, was the perpetrator of the crime. Unfortunately though, he couldn't be traced. Another option put forward by Mr Wood was that his client may indeed have been the perpetrator of the chilling scenes at Richmond Street, but could not be held responsible. He argued that Felix may have been so overcome with grief at the breakdown of his relationship with Mary Plain that he literally lost his mind and turned insane. For that a less severe verdict of manslaughter would be more appropriate. The judge did not agree.

'I'm afraid the jury can't consistently with the law bring in such a verdict, Mr Wood. The question that they must consider is whether the prisoner had voluntarily committed the cruel act of cutting the throats of the children'. In regards to the lodger, his Lordship added that he had more or less nothing to do with the case at all and his now untraceable particulars were not in the least bit suspicious. 'As strange as it may appear to you lawyers, people hate being called as witnesses in courts. If anyone heard of a murder having taken place in a house in which they were about to take lodgings, nine out of ten people would stay away. I cannot see any advantage in having the man had he appeared.' Continuing his summing up, the judge remarked that whether Mr Spicer liked children or not was totally irrelevant. 'Because a man was fond of children as pretty engaging little things did not mean he could not attack them when in a passion, and there is no evidence to suggest that the man was medically insane.'

Dr Fennell, medical officer at Knutsford Gaol, had been in charge of the accused while he had been incarcerated at the gaol. He had witnessed no sign of mental derangement or insanity within the mind of Felix Spicer. It was his opinion that he was of perfect mind, completely *compus mentus*.

The jury were sent off to deliberate and they left the court in an orderly and hushed fashion. Eight minutes of discussion revealed a unanimous verdict of guilty. His Honour held the menacing black cap in wait and Spicer began to tremble.

'Felix Spicer. You stand convicted of wilful murder. What have you got to say why the court should not give you judgement to die according to the law?'

'I am not guilty of the murder of my children my Lord. If I had worked on my own evidence I should have proved it to you. I gave Mr Wood some papers. If you were to read them you would exonerate me.'

'Felix Spicer.'

'Yes my Lord?'

'You stand convicted of wilful murder and that under circumstances as horrible as ever knew murder to be accompanied with. Mr Wood, at great labour to himself and sacrifice of much valuable time, has defended you with great skill and judgment ...'

'Yes, my Lord, I will admit,' protested Spicer, 'but if you had read them papers, if I had defended myself you would have given me a better verdict.'

The judge rubbed his face in irritable boredom. 'I cannot believe Mr Wood has not read your papers.'

'There are marks of blood on the stones where I cut my hands on the glass and on the windows.'

'That is exactly what Mr Wood has tried to persuade the jury. They would not believe it,' the judge answered.

Further last-minute reprieves were sought by Spicer, but all were rebuked as defunct nonsense. 'You have had a very skilled counsel but the jury have come to the conclusion that you are guilty of wilful murder. For my part I entirely share that opinion.' The judge finally adopted the black cap and without further delay issued the concluding death sentence.

The Home Secretary, Henry Matthews, a former QC himself, ruled against an appeal lodged on Mr Spicer's behalf and his sentence remained untouched. At Knutsford Gaol the sixty-year-old's life finally came to an end when he was hung from the end of James Berry's rope on 21 August.

GIVE UP THE GOAT

A peculiar case was presented at the Borough Police Court on 21 June 1884. Charles Gouldson, of 198 Beckwith Street, bore a grievance with William Renshaw and had summoned him before a borough magistrate.

Two years previously, Charles had purchased a young goat from a man named Mr Eastham. It was about seven months old at the time and Mr Gouldson kept the animal, worth 35s, in his garden. The goat had previously been in a scrap with a bulldog and now exhibited some distinctive bite marks on her nose. Eight months passed and it seemed as if the goat needed some company, so Charles took it to the dock fields where a few other goats were known to roam. 'I promised the men who were working at the place a few coppers for a drink for minding it,' Charles told the court. The previous Monday he had gone to the field to check up on his unusual pet and had discovered that she had given birth. Charles said that he had run around trying to catch the kid but it had proved too nimble for him. Later he found that his goat had been penned up and a policeman was called to investigate. The man was certain that the goat was his; he could pick it out from a thousand.

PC Wylie spoke with the owner of the pen, Mr Renshaw, and asked for an explanation. Renshaw told the constable that the goat belonged to him and that he had brought it about a year ago from a man who had since left town. 'I paid ten shillings for it,' he recalled, 'my daughter wanted goat's milk.' The defendant's wife and son both swore as to the goat being theirs. 'He brought it in April 1883. I remember because we married a month afterwards,' Mrs Renshaw attested.

Euphemia Breadon also gave evidence in support of the Renshaws. She said that she had often seen the animal passing to and from the defendant's house to the field by the docks.

Court assistants led the disputed beasts into the chamber and held them up to the magistrate. He peered forward and examined the goat's nose. The learned official noticed the very clear scars described by Mr Gouldson and he ruled in his favour.

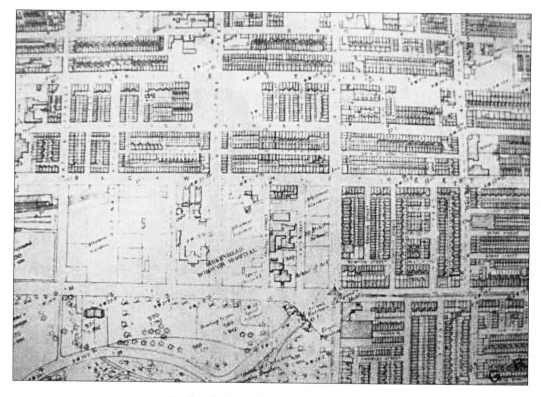

Beckwith Street shown in the late 1800s.

'But with regard to the kid, your worship?' asked solicitor Moore.

Solicitor Thompson spoke up in opposition. 'If it is the man's goat, it must be his kid also.'

'Complainant did not know it was with kid, and I should ask your worship to consider that this kid has been kept by the defendant for several weeks.'

'That has nothing to do with it,' tutted the magistrate.

Mr Moore looked shocked. 'The goat was kept at his house and required more than ordinary care. You have an equitable jurisdiction in the matter and ...'

He was cut short by a shrug of the magistrate's shoulders.

'What do you want me to do?'

'The defendant has been taking our milk all the time,' said Mr Thompson.

'No, the kid took all the milk', retorted Moore.

'The defendant tells you that he brought the goat for milk for his daughter. I submit that according to your worship's finding, we are entitled to the goat and kid.'

The magistrate was becoming noticeably confused. 'I do not see what you want done, Mr Moore. Is it a sum of money for the goat and the kid, or what?'

'Certainly, sir!' he smiled. 'The defendant has been at all the expense of the confinement.'

There was a slight pause. 'No, I cannot do that. I must make an order on defendant to deliver up the goat and kid forthwith.' The stipendiary then ruled in favour of Mr Gouldson.

Charles carried his goats from the court and received a number of bemused glances as he headed outside. A cab was hailed and he deposited the animals gently inside before departing home in triumph.

CAPTAIN PROWSE OF WHETSTONE LANE

On the evening of 31 January 1850, a most daring and outrageous robbery was committed upon a wealthy householder in Whetstone Lane, Birkenhead. Mr Prowse, a man who in his younger years had overcome many dramatic and dangerous storms during his long career at sea, was sitting in the front parlour of his home enjoying the calmness of his well-earned retirement. His doting wife was at his side. She was only too happy that her husband had survived such a perilous occupation as a sea captain and had earned enough

A map of Whetstone Lane, the residence of robbery victim Captain Prowse.

money for them both to live comfortably in a large well-furnished property with excellent views, and apparent security.

Mr Prowse relaxed back into his chair and took out his pipe. A few moments later the doorbell rang. The time was five minutes past seven and the elderly couple were not expecting any visitors. Prudence, their middle-aged servant, made her way down the hallway to answer the call as her employers sat waiting in the parlour. Prudence had no sooner unlocked the door when four or five men burst in at a frightful pace. Their faces were covered in rags with crudely cut eyeholes at the front. Another wore a crêpe mask. Two of the intruders pinioned the horrified maid by her arms and ordered her to stay quiet, but Prudence screamed as loud as her lungs would allow. The captain, on hearing the noise, got up from his seat in a most alarmed fashion and headed towards the parlour door. He reached for the knob, but before his wrinkled hand could take a firm grasp three figures burst into the room. They took hold of Mr Prowse, proving his bold resistance useless. He was thrown to the floor in a chaotic heave.

'Please do not murder him!' cried Mrs Prowse, as she stood sobbing against the far wall. One of the brutes swiftly came at the old woman and felled her wildly to the ground. She was quickly lifted up and a pistol was thrust hard into her tear-stained face. 'You will be shot if you dare scream,' snarled one of the men. Another of the gang members also brandished a pistol, and a third wielded a formidable bludgeon. The same threat was made to Mr Prowse and to Prudence, who had since been dragged into the parlour. The Prowses found themselves prisoners in their own home.

The three captives quickly realised that it would be downright idiotic, and possibly fatal for any of them to refuse the commands of silence. They agreed to stay quiet as the trespassers looked on smugly. Mrs Prowse was haphazardly searched and a small purse and a set of keys were handed over to one of the men, who appeared to be the ringleader. The scoundrel immediately emptied the ornate container but found it only housed half a sovereign and some silver. This was not enough. In a further act of gross disrespect the fiend placed his hand down her dress and began to rummage about her pockets. The woman stood shaking and pleaded that she had nothing more to give. Amongst the silver found in the purse was a 10s piece.

'This is not negotiable!' seethed one of the robbers as he threw the merge coin to the floorboards.

Mrs Prowse and her servant were forced into the dining room while the captain was ordered to hand over his keys and his own purse, which contained three sovereigns, several pieces of silver and a silver pocket watch.

Whetstone Lane in the twenty-first century.

The thieves began to help themselves to the wines and spirits, drinking copiously from the bottles. Mr Prowse was then brusquely marched up the stairs with several of the thugs following close behind. They demanded he open the cabinets and desks and they watched eagerly as the frightened old man pointed out the corresponding locks to the keys. Out of a writing desk emerged two £10 notes and a £20 note.

Downstairs two of the fellows were keeping watch over the women, and Mrs Prowse and Prudence were ordered to turn and face the wall. This they did and they stood heads down, pulses racing and with tears streaming down their faces. The laughing rogues proceeded to light candles and wondered about the house in a most brazen manner. The servant's room was ransacked and from within they discovered a rather plain purse containing a rather paltry £3. In their carnal pursuit of wealth the hoarders failed to notice a rather more attractive purse resting at the bottom of a trunk which contained a further £4.

In an upstairs bedroom the strain was beginning to get to Captain Prowse and he begged for a glass of water. His chest felt tight and his breathing had become heavy. In pain he struggled to inform his unwanted visitors where the kitchen was to get him a drink, but his humble request was ignored.

Several agonizing moments later the raiders decided to make their escape. They hastily ushered Mr Prowse back down the staircase and shoved him into the dining room with his fretful servant; his wife was sent to cower in the parlour. Seconds later the door was closed and an unmistakable metallic rattle was heard. They were locked in. The criminals had hurried down the hall fleeing the property from the rear.

The following hour witnessed the captain cutting away through the doorpost with only a small penknife in an ingenious bid to escape his newfound entrapment. Mrs Prowse attributed the noise made during her husband's attempted liberation in the next room to being that of the intruders. If she had only known that they had scarpered then she could have retrieved the key from the hallway and opened the dining room door. A further method of escape could have been the dining room window, but neither the captain nor Prudence realised that obvious option at the time; the evening's awful events having affected their presence of mind.

The police were immediately contacted and a scrupulous search of the neighbourhood was soon underway. It was thought that the burglars had attempted to commit a similar outrage the following evening. At a house in Clifton Park, a man was talking to his wife about the Prowse robbery when he was stopped mid-sentence by a succession of knocks. He went to answer it, merely opening the door a short distance with the security chain still in place. The visitor made a rush at him fully expecting the door to open. On finding it secure, the would-be crook stepped back and took on the guise of a vagrant, asking for any spare money.

The man shook his head and told the caller to go about his business and leave. He shut the door and turned. As he was about to return to the parlour he heard several voices coming from the front step before fading into the distance. The householder felt a lump in his throat. He realised that he and his wife may have been moments away from suffering the same fate as Mr and Mrs Prowse. The police issued stringent alerts across the town, but it is not known whether the perpetrators of theses daring outrages were ever caught.

A BULLET IN THE BRAIN

The cobbles of Conway Street tapped loudly beneath the heels of PC Sparrow as he walked his early morning beat. The sleepy Saturday morning of 9 December 1882 was relatively quiet, it still being only a quarter to six. In the distance walked Joseph Teece. PC Sparrow knew the man to be a provision dealer from Market Street, but just why he was walking about erratically in Exmouth Street at that time of the morning he wasn't able to tell.

'Officer! Officer!' Teece shouted. He had glimpsed the uniformed figure of PC Sparrow on the horizon and called out to him accompanied by an urgent oscillating wave. The constable hurried up the road to discover what on earth the matter was.

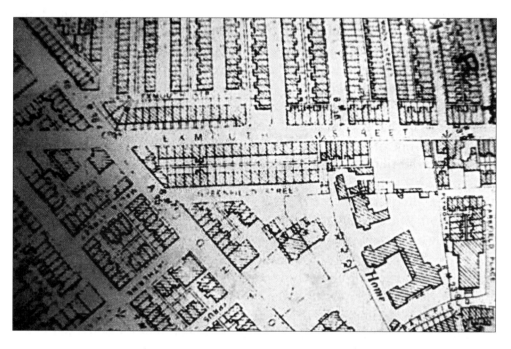

A map of Exmouth Street at the turn of the twentieth century.

'I need to be taken to hospital,' Teece wheezed. He was bleeding from two wounds, one on his forehead and another at the top of his skull. For several seconds the officer was lost for words. 'How ... how did that happen?' he stammered.

'Come on! I want to get there quick!' Joseph pleaded and he tugged Sparrow's arm. For some time Mr Teece refused to confess how he had sustained the suspiciously brutal wounds on his head but by the time they had met with doctors the dark truth was out. Joseph Teece had attempted suicide.

'I shot myself, and when I found the shots did not take effect I took some poison,' he said. A revolver was found in his pocket with two out of the six chambers being discharged. A small empty bottle labelled 'poison' was also discovered. Dr Brewer was most alarmed, and ordered the instant administering of a stomach pump and bandages.

Meanwhile, back in the town centre, Joseph's wife had made a frightful discovery and accosted a number of constables with some hysterical rambling in Watson Street.

'The servant! He has shot the servant girl!' she fretted.

The officers hurried to the Exmouth Street property, No. 36, and on Mrs Teece's direction burst into an upstairs bedroom. Jane Wrainwight was lying amongst the imbrued covers in a semi-conscious state. Her fringed forehead paraded a blackened bullet hole from which a stream of blood had trickled down her face. Fortunately for Jane the wound was steadily congealing with a sticky mass of plasma. Constable Sparrow knelt down at the bedside. 'Who did this to you?' he asked. Through Jane's almost unintelligible mumbles the policeman was able to hear one distinct and clear name: 'Joe.'

Neighbourhood physician, Dr Jennette, was awoken to attend the victim and exercise his medical talents in the hope of extending the poor domestic's ever-shortening lifespan. He had been Joseph Teece's consultant since September, the time when he had showed signs of *delirium tremens*, the symptoms of alcohol withdrawal.

On examining the girl he passed a petite medical instrument through the wound but could find no clear obstruction blocking the probe. The doctor mused for a few moments in silence. How far in had the bullet gone? He announced that he had no choice but to take the girl to hospital for a closer look at the damage, but he could not disguise his pessimistic tone. Death was surely only a matter of hours away.

On arrival at the hospital, Dr Jennette was able to acquire the use of a finer instrument and gently worked it into the bloodied wound in the woman's head. Four-and-a-half inches later, metal struck metal.

The area of Conway Street from where Joseph Teece was spotted by police in 1882.

In another room Joseph Teece was still under the strictest observations of Dr Brewer. He appeared to be suffering from the effects of the toxin he had confessed to downing some hours earlier and smelt strongly of chloroform. Attendants walked Mr Teece around the corridors to keep the poisoned patient from falling asleep and possibly slipping into a coma, or worse. At times his behaviour was anything but orderly and it took several pairs of strong hands to keep the man restrained. At one point Joseph became quite determined to seek out and find his intended kill. 'I wonder if she is in bed yet?' he hollered, and began to run around the wards pulling sheets from their matresses in search of Wainwright. 'Is there acid on the bandages? Have you put any on the bed?'

Dr Brewer acted fast and helped subdue Teece, keeping him under heavy control. 'What sort of acid?' queried the doctor, as he took Joseph firmly by the arm. 'Something that makes you delirious!' laughed Teece. It was all a rather worrying spectacle to the other patients, who had no choice but to lie in their beds in terror as a screaming Teece was led away down the hall.

The healing of the gunshot injuries sustained by both Teece and Wainwright was nothing short of miraculous in the days that followed, but Jane was also suffering from bouts of amnesia. She was able to recognise her relatives and eat small amounts of food, but if spoken to in the morning she would forget what was said by the afternoon. She did however recall playing dominos with

Joseph Teece on the Friday evening before the attack, but that was all.

By February both parties had sufficiently recovered from their injuries to face a court of law. Mr Teece was charged with feloniously wounding Miss Wainwright with intent to murder her, and with also having wounded her with intent to commit grievous bodily harm.

Jane herself was first to speak, if a little tentatively. She stated that she had been in the prisoner's employment for about five years and was reasonably happy working for the Teece household. As for being attacked, she could remember nothing. In fact the five days between her being shot and lying in hospital until the Wednesday were a total blank. For a number of days before the shooting, Jane told the court that Joe had been acting out of character, drinking heavily and not eating his meals.

'Do you know why that was?' questioned the defence solicitor, Mr Marshall.

'He was accusing people of trying to poison him,' the maid replied. 'On the day before the crime was committed he hardly spoke to anyone, and kept his head down, sitting beside the fire.' It was true that the accused was labouring under some severe form of paranoia. He held the unstoppable belief that a former friend was out to kill him after a falling out in London and that his life was in constant danger. Everyone was a suspect.

The judge asked if Mr Marshall intended to plead insanity as his client's defence, and, if so, to be aware that if convicted his client was likely be locked away for life.

'I am not responsible for the results my Lord.'

Dr Jennette told the court about his findings at the hospital and said that the bullet had gone in so deep that it could not be retrieved.

The judge lent forward to hear the details. 'Do you mean to say that she has a bullet in her brain?'

'I do. It is a very extraordinary case but still it is so,' answered the surgeon. 'The bullet had gone through the brain and is probably fixed in the bone.'

An independent practitioner by the name of Dr McEwan was called to prove that Teece had been suffering from the softening of the brain for some time, which perhaps played a part in his unusual behaviour. Mr Marshall knew that his client's best defence was insanity, but mental derangement rather than alcoholism at the time of the shooting was difficult to prove.

The jury retired to discuss the case in private. They duly returned with a guilty verdict for unlawful wounding, believing Teece to be in full control of his actions at the time of the attack. He was sentenced to twelve months imprisonment with hard labour.

THE MANIC TAILOR

On the afternoon of 29 April 1870, Mr James Dunlop a Liverpool tailor, left his residence in Highfield Park, Rock Ferry to visit a friend at Halewood Hall, near Runcorn. He had not been well for some time and felt a day or so away might do him some good. His journey there was completed with relative ease and the sixty-one year-old was soon at his friend's house, happy to be away from the pressures of life in Cheshire. After enjoying the somewhat muted remainder of the day the tailor retired to bed, but his mind began to race. No doubt the elderly tradesman endured a most troublesome slumber as the following day would see him attempt to commit a most frightful crime.

The next morning James got dressed and walked downstairs into one of the hall parlours. He had become bitterly depressed and wished to end his pain by any means possible. In the parlour James discovered a rather tempting double-barrelled gun and it just cried out to be used. With great agitation, Mr Dunlop retrieved some bullets, loaded the weapon and prepared to meet his end. Two shaking hands positioned the muzzle directly under his chin. It wouldn't be long now. He fired.

A loud crack echoed around the whole house and the room began to fill with a cloud of musty black smoke. Several servants rushed into the parlour to find their new houseguest standing in agony. The force of the discharge had caused the gun to kick back; the bullets merely sliced the tailor's lip and nose, completely missing any vital organs and failing in their deadly purpose. The smoking firearm was quickly taken from the bleeding man and medical aid was urgently sought. Mr Dunlop resisted. He frantically reached into his pocket and retrieved a penknife. With the utmost determination James flicked the blade open and began slicing through the flesh of his left arm. The servants looked on in horror as even more blood began to trickle onto the floor below. Slash after slash, the old man refused to give up his garish display of self-mutilation, until his energy finally began to drain away from him.

Dr Johnson soon arrived at the property and bandaged the wounds. His patient had at last calmed down and appeared to have overcome his distressing fatuous state of insanity. James was then put into a carriage and advised to go home and recover. The bandaged tailor sat utterly dejected in the cab. He did not wish to live. Somehow, with the last of his strength, Mr Dunlop summoned the energy to rip the dressings from his wounded arm and face. Yet more blood began to seep from his body and he suffered a severe bout of haemorrhaging. The driver, on realising the carnage in his cab, hurried to Liverpool where Dr Bickersteth, the tailor's former attendant, was contacted. Once again the wounds were bandaged and Mr Dunlop was given strict advice to go home and rest. The carriage had no sooner reached Rock Ferry when the old man's mood once again became twisted. With incredible violence the bandages were torn off a second time, exposing the deep and seeping wounds beneath. Doctors Spratley, Roper and Bickersteth attended the manic man at his home, but their combined efforts to save him were unavailing. At about twelve o'clock the following Thursday, James finally got his wish and died. At a subsequent inquest the coroner, Mr Churton, returned the verdict of death from acute mania and loss of blood.

AN EXPRESS SUICIDE

On 15 January 1883, an inquest was held into the circumstances of a most gruesome incident that took place aboard a Birkenhead-bound locomotive.

At the Victoria Hotel in Cleveland Street, Coroner Churton sat and mused over the unpleasant details surrounding the death of one passenger which took place on the previous Saturday evening. The first witness was Thomas Henry Evans, a wine merchant. He deposed that he had left the city of Chester by the 9.24 express train on the night of 13 January. As the train was nearing Bebington station, Mr Evans thought that he heard what sounded like a gunshot. It seemed relatively close by, possibly even in the next compartment to where he was sitting. The noise played on Thomas' mind and upon reaching Woodside he informed a porter, George Wilson,

Woodside railway station, where the body was finally discovered.

Bebington station, where the fatal gunshot was heard.

of his suspicions. Wilson escorted Mr Evans back aboard the train as he explained his fears. The porter investigated the carriages, one by one, until he came to one compartment with its door still shut. Wilson gave a gentle knock. There was no answer.

'Hello?' he called out, but again there was no response. He turned the handle and slid the door sideways. Wilson was met with a most ghastly scene. Inside the second-class carriage, beneath the speckled drawn blinds of the window, sat the mutilated corpse of a man. The majority of his face had been blown off by the large old-fashioned pistol which sat accusingly in the dead man's hand. Brain tissue was scattered all over the compartment and his black suit was heavily saturated with blood. The porter felt ill.

'A man has shot himself!' Wilson exclaimed. Thomas Evans peered around the doorframe to see what had happened. He too was taken aback at the appalling brutality which lay before him. He recoiled immediately but couldn't banish the stomach-churning image from his mind.

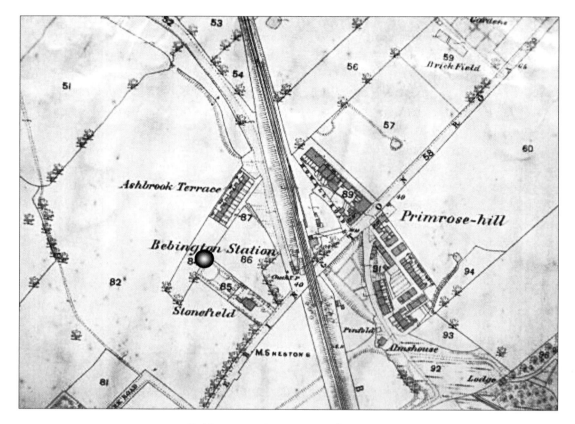

Bebington station on a map from 1875.

Mr Wilson himself was later called as a witness. He stated that upon finding the body at approximately 9.45 p.m. he had at once informed the station master, Mr Andrew. He recalled how he was ordered to find a doctor while Mr Andrew contacted the police.

PC John O'Neil described how, after arriving at the platform, he boarded the train and was shown to the compartment in question. The small window inside bore a hole the size of a sixpenny piece and it was clear that this was caused by the single bullet that had killed the man that now sat beneath it.

The constable recalled that the deceased was in his mid-thirties; about 5ft 9in in height, of slight build and had dark brown hair which was tinged with grey. The corpse had a whisker-style moustache and wore a smart black suit, brown socks and laced boots. PC O'Neil said that he searched the deceased's pockets and found upon his person £3, a small quantity of gunpowder, a number of lead pellets, some percussion caps and some bullets known as slugs. In the man's coat pocket sat a small bottle containing a sort of spirit.

This was also smeared with blood. The constable said that he could not find any papers or documents that would lead him to discovering the identity of the man; one of the few clues that could be found was the name of the manufacturer of his overcoat: Richardson & Co., Civil and Military Tailors at 179 Hockley, Birmingham. The constable then asserted that he ordered the body to be taken to the dead house in Watson Street.

There was another clue. Station Master Mr Andrew deposed how, upon learning of the origins of the alcohol bottle, he had sent a telegraph to the White Lion Hotel in Foregate Street, Chester. In their reply they informed him that the staff remembered a man matching the description given visiting the pub at about eight o'clock that evening. He was not local and had indeed purchased the aforesaid bottle of whiskey. Mr Andrew's meticulous research also yielded results about the origins of the dead man's weaponry. It seemed a Mr Jones, a gunsmith, returned a telegram stating that he had sold a pistol and powder to a man that sounded like the deceased at his shop in Northgate Street, Chester.

The jury listened intently and felt compelled to return a verdict of suicide, but there was no evidence to suggest the man's state of mind at the time. Coroner Churton directed that the internment of the body should be postponed for several days in the hope of identification. Later that week, several people from Birmingham contacted the Birkenhead authorities to inform them that they had links with the deceased and would leave for the Wirral at once to begin identification procedures. It is hoped that the body of the unknown man was reunited with those who knew and loved him best.

THE WRONG WINDOW

On Tuesday 17 February 1880, Margaret McEnvoy found herself in the dock facing a somewhat unusual charge. Mr Preston presided and the case was formally heard. The middle-aged Margaret spoke of how on the previous afternoon she had been out in Chester Street when the skies suddenly blackened, threatening a downpour. It soon began to rain quite heavily. In haste she headed into the Castle Hotel for shelter and, once inside, began chatting to two men who were enjoying a few drinks at the bar. They had seen that the woman had been caught in the rain and offered her a stiff drink to warm her up. She duly accepted and soon the conversation, and alcohol, began to flow. Patrick Driscoll took charge of the friendly dialogue. 'So what

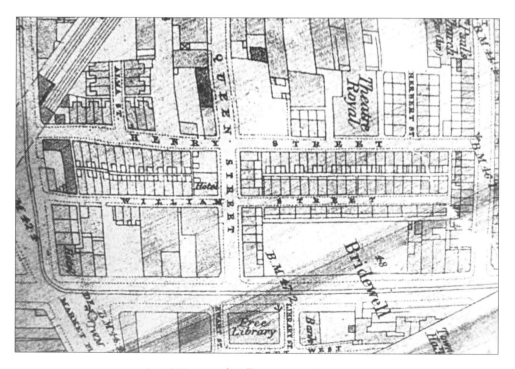

An 1875 map of William Street, Birkenhead.

do you do for a living?' he asked. Margaret told him that she was a servant but currently not employed, so made a living by charring.

'I want a woman to mind my children, and I'll pay you well to do it.'

The woman's eyes lit up. 'I wish I could get a situation like that, it's what I've been looking for, for I've been a housekeeper for a long time!'

'I have three children,' Patrick told her, as he took a quick sip of his drink, 'but they are very much neglected and I want a decent and respectable woman to look after them and keep them clean and nice.'

'Well you'll have a proper good housekeeper in me!' Margaret smiled excitedly.

Continuing, the jury listened to how the accused, after a few more drinks, left the Castle Hotel with Mr Driscoll and entered a house in William Street. There were three children in one of the rooms and they seemed pleased to see their father's new guest. Margaret introduced herself and informed the kids that their father had just engaged her to look after them and to keep them clean and tidy.

'Yes, we do want somebody; my sister wants a clean pinafore,' replied the eldest boy, 'the one she has is black and dirty.'

'Sit down and make yourself comfortable,' Patrick said, and she did. Not long afterwards Mr Driscoll went out and, according to Miss McEnvoy, did not return for about two hours, leaving her to look after his children on her own. She didn't mind, after all she was an experienced housekeeper and felt quite competent with the challenge.

On finally coming home Patrick was obviously very drunk and looking rather rough. Margaret then claimed her new employer had attempted to throw her down on a bed and have his way, but she was having none of it. At Margaret's rebuke Patrick allegedly kicked and beat her under an outburst of insults.

'Let me get out!' she shouted and with that she stormed out of the house. In a bitter rage she told the court that she had turned round and smashed a front window, gaining sufficient satisfaction for her gross mistreatment.

However, it was not Patrick Driscoll's window she shattered; it was Thomas Rudd's, his next-door neighbour. It was he who had reported Margaret to the authorities and who was pressing the charges that afternoon.

Mr Driscoll then took to the stand to defend himself of the accusations laid against him. He claimed that Miss McEnvoy was running after him all day and was so drunk that he couldn't get rid of her. Patrick said that when he came home at five o'clock he found her in his home sitting next to the fire combing her hair with his very own comb. He asked to know what brought her there and claimed he had never invited her in at all.

Mr Driscoll's former residence.

Whoever she was, she wouldn't shift. Patrick said that he shouted for his landlady and she too ordered the unwanted caller out. Margaret apparently argued, pleading that she was sorry and wished to make it up to him.

'Oh dear, what lies,' laughed Margaret sarcastically from her position in court.

The witness continued, claiming he himself had to place her coat on her and demand she be on her way.

In answer to the magistrate, Patrick said he had never taken or tried to take liberties with the woman and had certainly not thrown her on any bed whatsoever.

PC Wilson briefly took to the stand to confirm that Miss McEnvoy was very drunk when he was called to investigate.

Mr Preston remarked that the accused had a very bad character. She had been brought before the court approximately twenty-five times for various offences and had even been sentenced to five years penal servitude for her outrageous behaviour in 1872. Margaret McEnvoy was again found guilty, this time for the destruction of eight glass window panes. She was ordered to pay 4s 6d for the damage and a 40s fine, or face a month of imprisonment.

TAUGHT A LESSON

On the evening of 26 July 1904, eleven-year-old George Elliot was playing cricket with his two younger brothers and a friend in a field in Rock Ferry. After a few hours of fun and frivolity the boys decided to make their way home. The time was about eight o'clock and the summer sun was beginning to set. They walked up nearby Well Lane, playing a game they liked to call Follow the Leader. This involved the lads walking in a line and mimicking the person at the front. George was second in line and was enjoying being out with his friends in the warm summer air. This was true for many other kids right across the peninsula, as just yards behind the oscillating formation were three other children also taking in their last moments of sunshine. George and his friends continued on their way and happily tapped the gates and walls of the gardens that edged the pavement.

Just then George felt a swift sly slap across his right cheek. Over him stood Mr Herbert Edwards, schoolmaster of the training ship HMS *Conway*, and he was not amused. The boy was too shocked to say anything and continued walking, albeit a tad more briskly than before.

Typical youngsters playing in Well Lane, c. 1904.

A recent depiction of Well Lane, Tranmere.

'He had a cheek!' exclaimed George, safely out of earshot. The friends turned around and noticed that the three other kids who had been walking behind them were now in Mr Edwards' garden. The teacher stared up the road towards the group. 'You will get it!' he shouted angrily.

'Shut up!' George replied, practically spitting the words with guiltless wrath. Unfazed, George told his mates to keep walking and ignore what had happened. They travelled on for a few moments and began playing a game of cricket, before young Elliot again felt a smack across his already reddened face.

'What did you come into my garden for?' seethed Mr Edwards, his eyes squinting. The boy replied that he had not stepped foot in his garden and ran into the road to avoid another unnecessary blow. He tripped, sending the stumps rolling into the distance and scraping his bare skin against the cobbles. Mr Edwards bent down, picked up one of the stumps and began to beat the boy about his lower body with considerable force.

'It wasn't me sir!' cried George repeatedly.

'If it was not you then I will take it out of you,' bawled the teacher as he continued with his undue chastisement.

This abuse continued until Mr Brooks from Shakespeare Avenue, who had heard the screams, came over and remonstrated with the man. Mr Edwards ceased his disciplining. 'You devil! I will teach you to steal my flowers!' he yelled before storming off.

Mr Brooks and two or three passing people helped the boy lean against some railings and consoled him as best as they could.

Inspector Dean was contacted and he took the boy back to the house of Mr Edwards. The officer asked the schoolmaster whether he had hit the boy, a question to which he immediately admitted. 'He had been stealing my flowers!' he argued. George timorously denied he had been in the garden and said it was some other boys who he did not know.

'Where have the flowers been taken from?' enquired the inspector. Mr Edwards led the way into the front garden and showed the officer a section of his property were poppies were growing. Inspector Dean raised his eyebrows. He could not see any sign of a disturbance in the soil and to him the poppies there looked quite untouched. The officer reprimanded Mr Edwards and informed him that he should not have beaten the boy in any case. A neighbour who had been watching the goings-on came over to the garden. 'You have thrashed the boy unmercifully!' she declared. 'It made my heart ache to see how you thrashed him.' George's family were keen that Mr Edwards would not get away with treating him so cruelly and on 21 November had him brought before Judge Rowlands at the Birkenhead County Court. They were suing him for £50 in damages.

George, who now walked with a stick, had to be assisted into the witness box by his father. He explained to the court how he had been attacked so badly that Dr Knowles had to be called out to his home, 69 St Paul's Road, and prescribe for him.

For the defence, Mr Moore questioned the boy and it was heard how he had been forced to stay in bed for nine weeks to recover.

'When did you commence your holidays?' Mr Moore asked.

'I have been away from school for three months before 26 July because I had been ill-used the same by Mr Lobb, the schoolmaster at Mersey Road school.'

'Did you make a claim against Mr Lobb for that?'

'Yes, Sir,' answered George.

Mr Moore continued his interrogation. He suspected the lad to be a troublemaker and wished to paint this picture to the court. 'That case, I think,

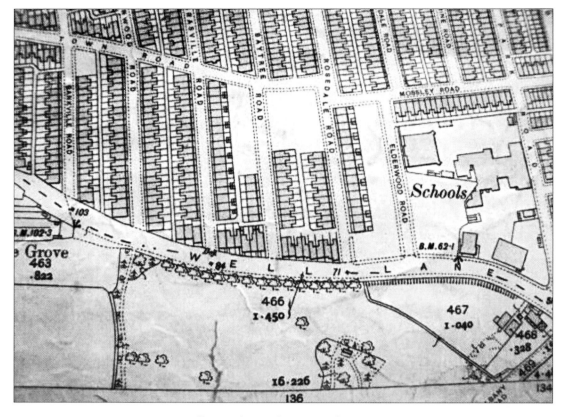

Well Lane depicted on a map from 1912.

was withdrawn on payment of costs and doctor's fees. Before that had you been at any other school?'

'Yes, St Paul's.'

'Was not your behaviour complained of there?'

The witness frowned defiantly. 'No,' he replied sharply.

Mr Brooks took to the stand and stated that he was walking about 200 yards from Victoria Park when he heard a scuffle going on, prior to which he had heard someone running. He said that he had turned around and saw the accused attacking the boy, George Elliot, with a stick. He ran towards them and ordered the defendant to stop. Whilst doing so he claimed Mr Edwards had lifted the boy by the neck before throwing him to the ground.

Dr Knowles attested that he had visited the Elliot household on 27 July and found George to be very restless and in significant pain.

'The right thigh had been injured – being contused, swollen and very tender to the touch. He must have received a severe punishment. His left shin was also bruised a little,' remarked the physician. He had attended his patient for about nine weeks and confirmed George had not been able to walk. Dr Knowles said that it would be some time yet before the child could bear any weight upon his leg and that he was certain it was a genuine set of injuries.

Dr Dalzell, who subsequently also examined Master Elliot, believed the patient to be in authentic distress, although it was his opinion that he was exaggerating the pain a little.

Dr Noble, Mr Edward's medical advisor, also examined the boy, with Dr Knowles in attendance.

'He complained of pain, but I could find nothing to show that he was in pain,' the doctor stated. The witness made him get out of bed and got him to stand. Dr Noble informed the court that the lad had told him that he couldn't move his leg, yet by various means the doctor was able to make him move without apparently causing any pain. 'If he had been in my care I would have risked sending him out.'

'You think he was shamming?' asked Judge Rowlands.

'Exaggerating I would say. I would not say he had no pain at all.'

Dr Dalzell agreed. When he had asked George to move his leg, he did not move it one inch. However, when distracted he moved his leg as high as anyone could and complained of no pain. This he achieved several times.

Mr Edwards himself was then questioned. He spoke of how he had been very annoyed of late due to the fact that bothersome children had been entering his garden and taking his flowers. He noticed the boys from his window and stood in the front room watching behind the curtains. A few moments later, Mr Edwards claimed he saw a boy with cricket equipment reach over from the side entrance and make a grab at some of his plants. 'I followed him and gave him half a dozen clouts,' confessed Mr Edwards. 'He looked like a dirty little rag-a-muffin that day, and I certainly did not pick him up in the way described and dash him to the ground.'

Then Elliot's solicitor, Mr Cotton, began probing.

'I suppose you don't feel very proud of yourself now do you?'

'I do feel proud of myself,' replied Mr Edwards pompously.

'Do you intend to justify this action in anyway?'

'I justify my defence of the action.'

Mr Cotton looked on aghast. 'At the moment I venture to hope that you feel ashamed of yourself?'

Mr Edwards' blood boiled. 'I am not ashamed of myself, I think *you* ought to be ashamed!' he shouted.

Mr Moore stated that he did not wish to justify the assault in anyway but that he would ask his Honour to say that the claim made was excessive and could the injuries be compensated by a more moderate sum? It certainly was a regrettable thing what the defendant had done on the spur of the moment, and there was no doubt he would have to pay in some way.

Mr Cotton interjected, stating that what had taken place was a mostly cowardly action by a full-grown man on a young boy, the worst he had ever heard.

Mrs Elliot, George's mother, expressed that she felt so angry at what the defendant had done to her son that she had issued a police summons, but when the officer had gone to serve it Mr Edwards was away relaxing on holiday. That was why no claim was made until 2 September.

Judge Rowlands had heard enough. It had been admitted that there was no legal justification for the beating and therefore the only question to answer was the amount of damages to be awarded. With regards to the medical evidence, his Honour remarked that it was unfortunate that doctors Dalzell and Noble were unable to examine the boy until so long after the event, about eight or nine weeks afterwards. Dr Knowles therefore was the person with the fullest knowledge of how severe the injuries were. The least amount of damages he could conscientiously allow was £40 and costs. In doing so the judge said he was taking a course which he was not quite sure was the right one, but hoped such a disgusting state of proceedings would never come before him at a civil court again.

THE FASHION THIEF

The ever-turning wheels of the Wirral justice system processed the remarkable case of a serial fashion thief back in the year 1884. George Morris was a nineteen-year-old rogue who had an unusual fascination with stealing clothes. Not just any old garments though – theatrical garments!

Mr Stanhope's Birkenhead Threatre in Priory Street was ransacked by the teenager, when he broke in and stole a number earrings, several breast pins, shoe buckles and, for some reason, an assortment of tights. Morris had gained

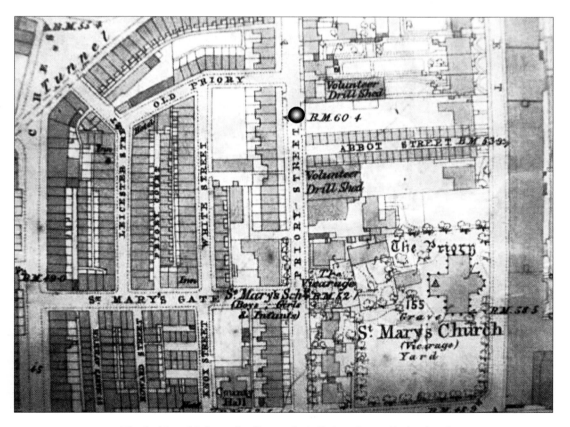

The fashion thief was finally caught in Priory Street, Birkenhead.

entry to the premises by crawling through the coal hole and once inside had forced open the internal doors.

On 13 May, Leigh Thomas' clothes store in Liscard was dealt a similar visit by the daring lad, but on that occasion George was embarrassingly caught in the act.

At a sitting of the Cheshire Quarter Sessions, George was tried for his thefts at Chester Castle on 30 June. The testimony of two boys who had spotted the accused at the scene of the crime on the early morning of 24 April, along with additional testimonies regarding George's disposal of a pair of tights and brazen procession of several pieces of the stolen articles, secured his guilt. Six months of imprisonment was deemed sufficient, along with a stylish and chic prison uniform.

AN UNSPORTING DRINKER

On the night of Monday 16 April 1894, Charles McHugh left his home in Cavendish Park to go out for a few drinks. The dock worker, who was well respected by most who knew him, walked around to Prenton Road East and paid a visit to the Sportsman's Arms at about ten o'clock. Charles walked over to the counter where he stood with two friends and ordered some beer. To Mr Orme, the manager, it seemed the conversation was of quite a friendly nature and he certainly did not expect to see his latest customer throw several

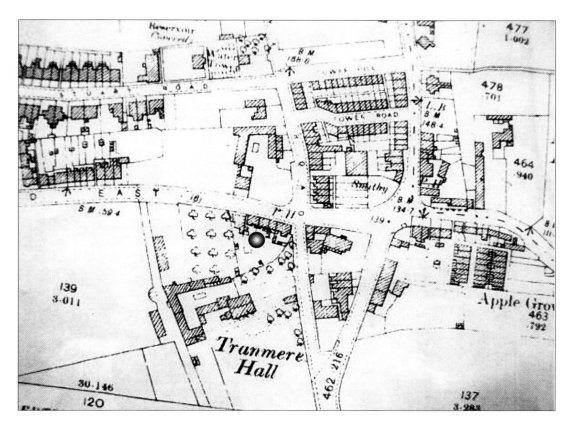

An 1899 map of Tranmere, showing the location of the pub in Prenton Road East.

The Sportsman is still a prominent feature in the Tranmere area.

hard punches upon one of his drinking companions, but that's exactly what happened.

Mr Orme immediately raced round to the public side of the bar and demanded that Charles leave the premises at once. 'I will finish my beer first!' he retorted. The manager repeatedly asked Mr McHugh to get out but it was of no use. A policeman was sent for and soon PC Cook arrived at the establishment. He had been at home at the time of the nocturnal assault and was still attired in his slippers. PC Cook had known the offender since he was a child, for about fourteen years or more. 'You had better finish your drink and leave or I shall put you out,' said the constable. Charles took no notice. 'If you lay your hand on me you'll never lay your hand on another man.'

Refusing to leave or even drink his beer, PC Cook forcibly took the glass from him. At this Charles became infuriated and grabbed the policeman by the throat. A struggle ensued which ended in Mr McHugh being forcibly ejected from the pub. Outside the constable attempted to calm Mr McHugh, but found himself being attacked yet again. He continued trying to persuade Charles to quieten down and go home. He really didn't want to have to arrest a personal friend but in the end the constable was forced to contact Inspector Allison and take the drunkard to the bridewell.

The following day Charles McHugh was brought to the Borough Police Court on the charge of being drunk and disorderly, refusing to quit the premises of Licensee Thomas Matthews, and for assaulting Constable Cook in the execution of his duty.

Charles admitted refusing to leave the premises and apologised for his violent conduct the previous evening. The constable stated that he did not wish to press charges for the treatment he had received from the accused, and Mr Orme stated that to him Mr McHugh appeared not to be drunk, but merely agitated.

The Bench believed the prisoner to have caused a great deal of trouble and PC Cook had shown great forbearance with him, as such behaviour jeopardized the license of the establishment. Mr McHugh had been in court before but it had been some years ago. It was hoped he would not be seen again for some time yet, hopefully never. Charles McHugh was fined 40s plus costs.

A SENSITIVE WOMAN

A most tragic inquest was held by Mr Cecil Holden on the afternoon of 15 October 1913. The subject of the proceedings was Mrs Amy Richardson, who had committed suicide on the previous Tuesday. At about seven o'clock on the Monday night, Mrs Richardson was rushed into the Borough Hospital suffering from carbolic poisoning. It had been self-administered and she died shortly afterwards. The coroner began outlining the terrible circumstances to the jury.

The first realisation of the tragedy was deduced by the deceased's husband, PC James Richardson. On returning home to 35 Sun Street, Birkenhead, at about six o'clock, his little daughter came down the stairs to greet him.

The vicinity of Sun Street, as seen in 2009.

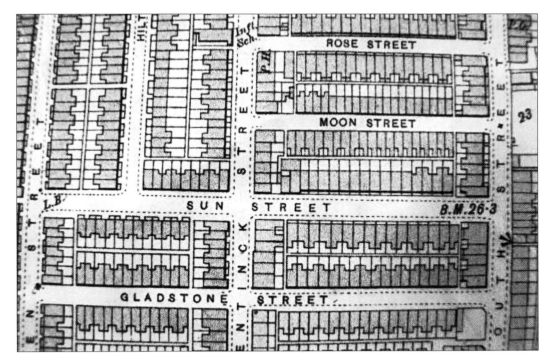

The Richardson's residence, Sun Street.

'Whatever is the matter with mamma dad?' she asked tearfully. Mr Richardson hurried up the stairs and to his horror found his dear wife unconscious on the bed and making an odd gurgling sound. He could smell carbolic acid and it soon occurred to James that he had noticed a bottle of carbolicene and a cup sitting in the parlour. It had been in the house for as long as he could remember and was usually only used as a disinfectant. Thinking fast, the distraught constable administered an emetic of mustard and water before sending for an ambulance. Under the pillow he found a heartbreaking note, Amy's last words. It read:

Dear Jim,
Goodbye and God bless you and my little children. Get Nellie and Cissie to look after them. I'll be trouble to nobody and they can't skit at me anymore, for there is some treachery but I cannot fathom it out, but keep your neighbours out of the house. What has to come out will out. Perhaps Mrs Reeves will tell you, for I don't know. I've been watched enough.

The coroner added that the note also included several verses of hymns.

PC Mitchell stated that he was on duty in Watson Street at the time of the incident and was called to recover the evidence.

Dr Brown, junior house surgeon at the Borough Hospital, stated that Amy was brought to him on Monday evening and that he could immediately smell the carbolic acid on her body. It was a hopeless case.

PC Richardson spoke of how recently in the course of his duty he had been forced to summon some youths near to his home for disorderly conduct. Since then the lads had been jeering and worrying his wife and he thought they had upset her. James had repeatedly told her not to be concerned, but Amy continued to worry so much as to make herself ill.

Jim confessed that recently his wife had mentioned something about looking at his razors but on thinking of their children thankfully decided against doing anything rash. James sobbed that he did not think to hide them from her as he did not believe she was so depressed.

Mrs Reeves, as mentioned in the note, was questioned and she told the inquest that she had been a friend of the deceased for two years. On the Monday she had complained to her of a headache but not once did Mrs Richardson ever mention any trouble with her neighbours. 'She was a very sensitive woman,' said Mrs Reeves.

A Mrs Owens deposed that she also knew the deceased woman, had never had any trouble with her and knew of no attempts by anyone trying to make Amy's life a misery. The woman's apparent suicide was totally out of the blue.

James recalled solemnly that his wife had said to him many times that she wished that she was dead and that she would take their children with her. How he wished he had listened.

The coroner, Mr Holden, in summing up said that there was sufficient evidence to show that Amy Richardson committed the act whilst she was insane. The point was whether or not she was interfered with by the neighbours.

The jury deliberated and returned a verdict that the deceased died from paralysis of the heart consequent on taking carbolicene which was self-administrated. They also held the view that at the time she was temporarily insane and tendered their deepest sympathies to James and his children.

THE CASE OF HENRY CODDINGTON

You're killing me! Murder!' These were the chilling words which fell upon the ears of PC Oldham as he walked his nocturnal beat along the bottom of Clifton Park, Tranmere. It was New Year's Eve 1869 and further menacing cries commenced to shriek out, 'You'll kill me! Murder!' The constable sped in the direction of the screams, female screams, and was immediately stopped by two women. One of the women, Margaret Weston of Austin Street, breathlessly informed PC Oldham of a terrible incident she had just witnessed nearby. Miss Weston said that she had seen a man and a woman arguing in the street. The woman wanted to walk up Clifton Park but the man refused, shouting at her and saying that they were going to go down Borough Road instead. The policeman listened to Margaret's account and learned that she had also heard the chilling cry of murder and unsettling screams. PC Oldham hastily thanked the witness for the information and went off in search of the couple in question. Moments later the constable was joined by Thomas Lightbound, a conscientious local who had also heard the trouble. Together they spotted a woman sitting on the pavement and a man leaning over her. They were Sarah and Henry Coddington, and they were obviously arguing. Mr Coddington was a negro bus driver and had been known to PC Oldham for several years.

'Who is she?' the constable asked him, having never come across the woman before. 'She is my wife,' replied Henry. 'We have been having a bit of a quarrel.' The woman appeared to be drunk so both PC Oldham and Henry were forced to help lift her from the ground and endeavoured to get her on her feet. 'I'll not go,' she slurred. Mrs Coddington seemed to have lost the use of her legs and hung between the men like a piece of lead. They managed to get Sarah a few yards up the road, almost carrying her, before she suddenly pulled away. 'I will not go with him!' she screeched. 'He has kicked me like a dog and I am bleeding,' she cried, before settling down on the roadside. In the darkness PC Oldham could see no obvious injury. 'Get up and try to go with your husband,' he ordered, but it was no use. 'I'll go by myself,'

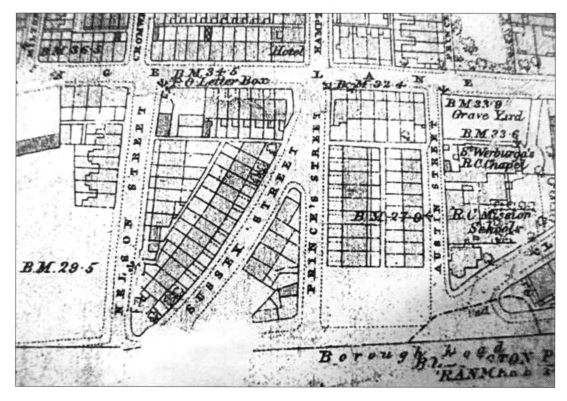

The area of Borough Road where Mrs Coddington recieved her fatal injury.

retorted Sarah, before heaving herself up, crossing the road and staggering off into the distance. Henry calmly chased after her and they headed off in the direction of Sussex Street. The constable and Mr Lightbound returned to the spot where they had first seen the Coddingtons and struck a match to help them see. The warm orange glow revealed a horrific puddle of blood where Mrs Coddington had been sitting. More spots of blood were found trailing up the pavement which led the two men, along with Mr McDowell who had also witnessed the incident, to Mr and Mrs Coddington, where her condition was assessed. The constable found that she was in no fit state to return home and on his orders a car was sent for her to be taken to the Borough Hospital. During the journey Henry comforted his wife as best as possible and to the officer appeared to be nothing more than a loving and doting husband.

On arrival, Dr Vacher examined the woman. Her face and neck were very much blanched and her legs were covered in blood. The doctor discovered that she was bleeding from the vulva, to which he applied a compress.

Once done, Dr Vacher gave Mrs Coddington a quantity of brandy. Sadly, she had haemorrhaged so severely she died only ten minutes later.

PC Oldham was informed of the findings and Henry Coddington was immediately arrested on suspicion of inflicting the fatal injuries and taken into custody. 'It's a bad job,' Henry whimpered, seeming very much distressed. Mr Coddington himself had had a drink, but the constable did not believe him to be drunk.

The following Tuesday, Dr Vacher conducted a post-mortem upon the deceased. He found the body to be in a generally healthy and well nourished state, but very much blanched from a great loss of blood. Further to this a bruise upon the right buttock was discovered, as well as a graze to the left knee. In the anterior wall of Mrs Coddington's vagina there was a lacerated wound in the shape of an inverted 'V' approximately three inches in length, but not of much depth. The other parts of the body were in fine order, except the kidneys. There was no doubt in Dr Vacher's mind that haemorrhage was responsible for the woman's death.

An inquest was held before Mr Churton at the Queen's Hotel on the morning of 3 January. The jury, having visited the Borough Hospital to view the body, sat to hear the details of a possible case of murder.

Marcella Price stated that she lived with her husband at 19 Warwick Street and rented apartments from the prisoner, Henry Coddington. She had seen the body of the deceased and had identified it as that of her landlady. Mrs Price alleged that Mrs Coddington's had been addicted to drink and was often under the influence, causing her to have a rather quarrelsome disposition.

The jury heard how the when the deceased argued with her husband she would often use most shocking language towards him. She had also pledged almost every article in the house and, lately, their children had been running about practically naked. By all accounts Mrs Coddington was violent towards her husband.

James McDowell, of Clifton Park then gave his version of events:

I was going from my own house to Birkenhead on Friday evening last, about a quarter-past eight o'clock, when I met a man and woman in Borough Road. The man was going fast and the woman was close behind. They were talking rather loudly and I heard the prisoner say, 'Come on' in an authoritative tone. After I had passed them about forty paces I turned and saw them both on the ground struggling. I heard the woman give out a groan as if she had been hurt. Thomas Lightbound then appeared whilst I stood there and I remarked to him that I was afraid that there was some foul play going on.

After hearing further details from PC Oldham and Margaret Weston, the inquest was adjourned until 5 January, when evidence from a previously unknown witness was uncovered. Edward Richards, a draper's assistant of 71 Hamilton Street, took the stand and told the court how, on the night in question, he had been going down Borough Road at about half-past eight when he heard someone cry out several times, 'You've killed me!' On hurrying to the spot he found Henry Coddington half-carrying a woman. On seeing the witness, the woman reached out to him and pleaded, 'If you are a gentleman you will take me from him. He has kicked me and I am bleeding to death.'

Mr Richards said that he had asked the man if the woman was his wife. Henry replied that she was and requested the witnesses' help in escorting his spouse home. Edward did this for a few yards but soon noticed a policeman approaching with another man, so decided to leave them to it. The draper's assistant was adamant that he did not consider the woman to be in any danger. On the contrary, Mrs Coddington did not seem weak at all and spoke with a very loud, deep voice. If he had known the true extent of the danger that the woman was in, Edward was adamant that he would have done more for her.

Sarah did not appear so drunk at the time, yet the man appeared to be doing all he could to get her home. 'You all know the darkey that drives the buses,' she bawled, and then added, 'you'll see it in the paper in the morning.'

Cross-examined by Mr Betherton for the defence, Edward Richards was brought to task over his apparent carelessness.

'I did not speak to the officer as I did not think there was anything serious about the affair,' answered Mr Richards. 'I did not speak to the woman and I didn't observe any signs of her being in drink.'

Samuel Price, a whitesmith lodging at the prisoner's house in Warwick Street, was questioned next. He deposed that he saw the deceased at about seven o'clock on the Friday evening with her husband on their way to chapel. They appeared to be on friendly terms and to Samuel, Mrs Coddington did not seem to be in liquor. According to Mr Price the deceased was a woman of intemperate habits and had a violent temper towards her husband. 'He always treated her kindly,' said Samuel, 'but she would often, when he would come home late, refuse to let him in and have no tea ready.'

Dr Vacher was questioned by a juror regarding the cause of the vaginal wound found on Sarah's body. The doctor replied that it may have been caused by a kick, or by a fall on a sharp stone. The physician stated that Henry's boot, which he produced, could well have inflicted the blow, but he was not certain. The wound may have been caused by Mr Coddington drawing his foot suddenly from under his wife while she was sitting or lying on the ground. Indeed Mrs Coddington was thinly clad and the kick might have been inflicted outside the petticoat, which would account for the lack of bruising on the thighs.

Mr Bretherton then addressed the jury on behalf of the accused. He described the deceased as an abusive and intemperate woman, while her husband was quiet, industrious and inoffensive. 'On Friday night the deceased behaved most abusively toward him, but he, both before and after this occurrence, was calm, gentle and patient towards her,' said the solicitor. He added that if his client had indeed kicked Mrs Coddington, as previously alleged, then there would have been more marks of violence on her body. Furthermore, there was actually no solid evidence of kicking at all, and who would trust the words of a drunken woman in a passion? 'There is nothing to combat my own theory that the deceased fell on a sharp stone and the fall itself was the cause of the medley, not the accused,' concluded Mr Bretherton.

The coroner, after summing up the evidence put before him, asked the jury to retire and to consider a verdict. The jury consulted in private and after fifteen minutes reached a unanimous decision. 'The deceased came by her death from haemorrhage caused by a wound in the vagina, but there is no evidence to show how that wound was caused,' declared Mr Getley, the foreman.

The jury was then discharged and the prisoner taken to Abbey Street to await trial before magistrate Mr Preston the following Thursday. The evidence heard at the inquest was repeated, but since that day a new witness had come forward. Harold Reeves, an apprentice architect of Chestnut Grove, Tranmere, recalled how he had been in the yard of St Werburgh's Chapel at about eight o'clock on the night in question. He stated that he had seen the accused and his wife and that she was very drunk and lying on the ground. Mr Coddington was attempting to help but she only responded with a vile string of obscenities. Mr Reeves told the court he had observed the couple heading towards Borough Road and the last thing he witnessed was in fact Mrs Coddington trying to kick her husband.

The magistrate deliberated and came to the conclusion that the case was too severe to be dealt with by a local court. If was therefore decided that the prisoner would be sent to Chester to stand trial at the assizes on the charge of manslaughter. The Bench fixed Mr Coddington's bail at £100. Mr Rathe, landlord of the Tabot Inn, Oxton, and Mr Healing, manager of the Great Western Railway goods department were accepted as securities. The weight of the situation was having a crushing effect on the defendant's mind. It became clear to officials that Henry was becoming slowly but surely

St Catherine's Church shown in the distance on Church Road.

deranged. A policeman remarked that Henry repeated several times to him that his stomach was full of electricity, and Dr Vacher witnessed signs of severe mental anxiety. Based on these warnings, arrangements were made to have Henry locked up at the Union Workhouse. Thomas Evans, Mr Coddington's previous employer, arranged a cab to convey him there. A sympathetic crowd of people waited outside the bridewell and gave the accused a hearty cheer of support as he drove off.

The following day Mr Coddington seemed much better and in a rational sate of mind. The weekend however saw Henry act most unlike his usual self, taking very little food or sleep. On Sunday morning Governor Redding allowed his new inmate out into the garden at the front of the workhouse. The garden was enclosed by a strong iron railing measuring about 5ft in height. Accompanied by two wardens, Henry walked calmly around the garden taking in some fresh air seeming perfectly *compus mentus*. But in an instant Henry darted away from the wardens and with acrobatic skill scrambled over the fence and ran towards the gates. The ex-bus driver shook them hard, but the gates were well and truly shut. Before he had a chance to climb over to Church Road Henry was secured by two wardens and the governor. 'Where were you going, Mr Coddington?' asked a warden politely.

'I was only going down to Birkenhead,' replied Henry.

St Catherine's Church, with the workhouse in the background.

During the afternoon Henry's mood was most devotional and he prayed for about three hours in a loud, deep voice, crying insensibly throughout. His sobbing was so fierce the congregation at nearby St Catherine's Church had their own prayers disrupted.

On the following Monday morning, while in the dormitory on the ground floor and attended by two members of workhouse, Henry suddenly bolted towards the door. This was locked but the large fan light above it, at a height of between 6ft and 8ft, was open. With surprising agility he scrambled through the opening and fell out into the main corridor before running through to another dormitory. In this room sat an open window and it was through this that Henry jumped, bringing him into the exercise yard and the great gates of the porters lodge at the rear of the building. These gates were surmounted with large iron spikes but the absconder had no qualms in attempting to overcome these with his previous athletic skill. On climbing over the gates Henry severely injured his right hand and dislocated his ankle falling down the other side. This misfortune gave several pursuing wardens the chance to finally grab hold of the inmate and take him back inside to attend his injuries.

Staff who frequently spoke with Mr Coddington stated that he seemed perfectly fine when talking about everyday matters, but became exceedingly irrational and unhinged when discussing what led to his incarceration and

The view from St Werburgh's Church, looking up Borough Road, 2009.

the charges which hung over him. He claimed to see his wife every night and told them how he longed to talk with her; he would then accuse the wardens of making the charges up and stated that he would be with her before long. At other times wardens heard Henry ramble about not killing the Pope and that he wouldn't do such a thing, nor kill a bishop either, and that it wasn't fair that he should be sent to Chester for doing it. On discussing his children, all five of whom had since been placed in schools belonging to the Union, Henry would appear quite sensible and express wishes to see them again.

On Sunday the workhouse chaplain, the Revd Tattersall, spoke to Mr Coddington but was not well received. Henry requested to speak with Canon Chapman of St Werburgh's Roman Catholic Chapel instead, and he found great relief in speaking with the man of the cloth. The governor held the opinion that if only Mr Coddington would eat and sleep more then he would soon be alright. If not, then perhaps a cell at Chester Asylum was needed.

Fortunately, Henry's mood remained stable enough for him to remain in his current institution until his trial at the assizes. On Thursday 7 April, before Sir William Bovill, Henry Coddington stood trial on the charge of manslaughter. The evidence heard before the magistrate was reaffirmed, with the conclusions of Dr Vacher being paramount to the case. On giving evidence he stated that the deceased may have suffered the injuries that were found upon her by falling on a sharp stone. At this Mr Parkins for the prosecution proceeded to ask why such damage could not have been inflicted by a boot.

The judge at this point interjected, 'The witness might as well be asked whether it had not been caused by a post.' His Lordship continued, stating that if the prosecution had proof that the prisoner kicked the deceased in that manner, then such a question could be justified. There was no proof in the depositions that Mr Coddington had kicked his wife and in fact the evidence showed that he had behaved most affectionately towards her.

'There is the deceased's statement,' quickly answered Mr Parkins.

Under cross-examination Dr Vacher said that the wound might have been caused by a fall upon on a stone lying irregularly on the ground, or if a man and woman fell down, the man, in trying to extricate himself, might possibly cause it.

After some further evidence, His Lordship asked Mr Parkins whether he could produce any solid evidence that Henry had assaulted his wife on the night in question. He could not.

'Then it is idle to go on with this case!' scoffed the judge, before directing the jury to acquit Mr Coddington of the charges against him. The news was met with great relief not only by Henry, but by his many supporters in the courtroom and back home in Birkenhead.

SWINE CRUELTY

On 20 May 1879, Inspector Luckings of the RSPCA made his way to 3 Wallasey Dock's slaughterhouse to carry out a surprise inspection. It was about half-past nine in the evening and the place was still in operation with workers busily engaged in the business of meat production. The bloodcurdling sound of squealing swine pierced the night air, but this was the hard truth of the industry and Luckings was used to it. The inspector took a good look around but was a little surprised by the lack of light. He soon came across one pen which was in almost darkness, but Inspector Luckings could just about see what was going on from a gas light hanging approximately 30ft away. Inside the pen was a man called Hugh Landy, a somewhat dim-witted member of staff who got a cheap thrill out of his unenviable job. He was with two other workers, Thomas Wilson and William Utley, and they obviously shared the same mental disposition as Landy. Inspector Luckings could see that they brandished long poleaxes; a heavy stick to which the sharp blade of an axe head was attached at one end. This wasn't the normal way to

The former Wallasey Dock is still a busy shipping hub.

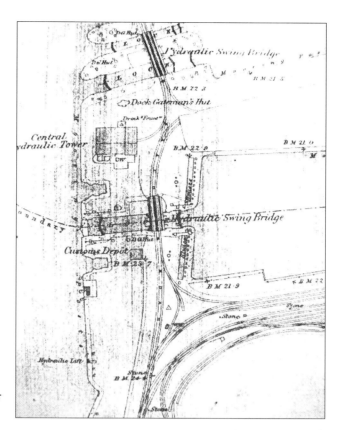

*A contemporary map of
Wallasey Dock.*

slaughter pigs. Usually the animals were separated and stunned before being killed and taken away professionally, but Landy and his colleagues proceeded to strike the pigs at random with their weapons, sending them running in an escapeless frenzy. The pen was only 30ft by 20ft and held about thirty petrified pigs; the number dropping with every hit. Worse still, they only struck once before looking for the next victim, leaving the poor animal hollering in pain. Sometimes a blade struck sideways, tearing open the animal's underside and causing blood and guts to spill out onto the filth-ridden floor of the pen. The inspector could watch no more and called an end to the malicious events of the slaughterhouse and had the three fellows charged with cruelty. William Utley was supervisor and he was less than impressed with the interference of his fun. He became most abusive and caused quite a scene when remonstrated with. Nevertheless, on 25 June, Landy, Wilson and Utley where summoned to the Petty Sessions and found guilty of the charges laid against them. Landy and Wilson were each fined 40s plus costs, while the disorderly Utley was ordered to pay £5 including costs.

THE TROUSER THIEF

In April 1870, landlady Ann Morgan took in a late-night lodger by the name of William Richardson at her house in Beckwith Street. A few days later William left, taking with him a pair of trousers belonging to a fellow lodger, Mr Thompson. With the crime occurring under her own roof, Mrs Morgan felt compelled to inform the local police of the theft. Posters were printed offering a reward for information regarding the missing trousers, but this was to no avail. The sixty-year-old was so eager to track down the trouser thief that she approached a lady by the name of Elizabeth Steers at her home in Chester Street. Elizabeth was known to be a fortune-teller and Mrs Morgan wondered whether she may be able to help in her criminal-catching exploits. She asked Mrs Steers if she could fathom any information regarding the whereabouts of Mr Richardson and the property he had stolen. Elizabeth mused solemnly, and then calmly placed an intriguing crystal ball on the table in front of her.

'A shilling please,' asked Mrs Steers. This was her usual fee for such consultations. Elizabeth grasped the crystal ball in her bony hands and handed the unusual sphere to Mrs Morgan. 'No, no,' Ann exclaimed as she shook her hand from side to side. She did not wish to handle any such items. Anything could happen.

Mrs Steers instead placed the crystal ball back onto the small table between the pair and began staring deeply into its centre. A few moments of silence passed and it seemed for a minute or two as if the woman's crystal was broken.

'Look!' cried Elizabeth with an unexpected jolt. Catching her breath Ann slowly peered forward, hoping to catch a glimpse of her former tenant within the glass's cloudy interior.

'Can you see the man?' gasped Mrs Steers.

Ann squinted hard, but no, she could not. However, it did appear that there was something inside the occultist's object. The landlady couldn't quite make out what it was, but it was definitely not a man.

Elizabeth suddenly took hold of the globe and held it dramatically in her palm. She said that she would now interpret what she called her five revelations of destiny.

Beckwith Street, as seen in 2009.

'The man who has stolen the trousers is a stout man of dark complexion.'

Mrs Morgan's stomach filled with butterflies. 'Oh?' she asked eagerly. This matched her memory of William Richardson.

'He is in Liverpool!' continued Elizabeth, 'and if you go in search of him he will be found. Go along the street past the Exchange and beyond the railway bridge. On the first turning on the other side you will find the man.'

Ann could hardly contain her excitement. She thanked the fortune teller and left the house at once to commence her search.

Several hours passed and much to Mrs Morgan's dismay she could find no trace of the culprit whom she had so desperately wanted to find. Feeling that she had been duped, the rather embarrassed woman went to the police.

Detective Hemmingway of the Birkenhead Police listened to her story and then made his way to Mrs Steers' house in Chester Street to make some enquiries.

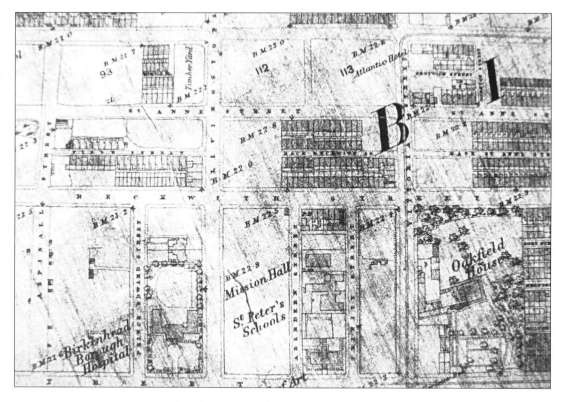

Beckwith Street on a late nineteenth century map.

'Have you found the man?' asked Elizabeth.

'No we have not,' answered the detective.

On hearing the news Mrs Steers pulled out a mysterious black bag. The officer looked on bemused.

'Reach into this and you shall pull out the name of the thief,' smiled Elizabeth. With raised eyebrows Detective Hemmingway reached in deep and retrieved a small crystal ball.

The officer sighed. He was not a believer in all this mumbo-jumbo and all that he could foresee was Mrs Steers locked in a police cell. He charged the old woman with obtaining money under false pretences and took her to the Town Hall bridewell. The detective had heard about Mrs Steers and her trickery before and knew of several naïve servant girls who had been caught out in the same way. One half-witted girl named Curtis had had a number of possessions stolen from her home and consulted the woman, paying her half a crown. Mrs Steers felt no guilt in telling the girl that her next-door neighbour had committed the thefts and in consequence a great deal of trouble had taken place within the neighbourhood. Mrs Steers was a troublemaker!

On the afternoon of Monday 7 March, Magistrate Mr Preston resided over the case. After hearing the evidence it was his view that Mrs Steers was guilty of the charge laid against her and he could not in good conscious allow people to be duped out of their money in such a mischievous manner.

'It is extraordinary that in the nineteenth century there should still be such fools as to believe such things,' laughed Mr Preston sarcastically. 'Prisoner must go to gaol for a month.'

THE RIVALS

In the late nineteen century there stood a certain property in Birkenhead's Argyle Street. It housed two artistic rivals whose jealousy and bitterness would inevitably bring them both before a court.

The trial of William Staples, a photographer, was held before Mr Preston at the Town Hall in February 1870. He had had charges pressed against him by Adolphe Koenigsberger, a picture dealer who was claiming £4 15s in damage to his property.

Mr Moore, appearing on behalf of Mr Staples, stated that his client had a studio situated over the shop of the defendant in Argyle Street. It was no secret that William was annoyed that Koenigsberger sold carte-de-viste frames downstairs; a product that he also sold from his studio upstairs. William admitted that he would often make disparaging remarks to his commercial rival, but that there was no real malice intended.

Adolphe Koenigsberger claimed that on 11 January he arrived at his shop at about half-past ten in the morning. On arrival his young employee, a lad by the name of Yapp, told him that there had been some heavy knocking coming from upstairs. Before he could finish his sentence the noise started again. It sounded as if someone was jumping from a high stool or table and the whole shop shook. Mr Koenigsberger recalled how suddenly there was a loud crack and a number of pictures and frames fell from the walls, several ornaments smashed from their shelves and two glass globes plummeted from the chandelier. As soon as the destruction was heard the jumping ceased.

There were further unusual vibrations intermittently throughout the day, each causing even more damage to Adolphe's carefully-positioned stock. The house was very lightly built and there was much vibration from passing trains, but none had ever caused anything to fall or to be knocked down in the past.

The court heard how Mr Staples would often hurl abuse at the claimant, shouting 'pumpen-musser' and other such insults. Mr Koenigsberger alleged that the defendant also told his landlord that he kept prostitutes and had informed the Alliance Insurance Co. that his stock wasn't worth what it was insured for.

Birkenhead's Argyle Street, 2009.

On the 19th it was alleged how there had been more commotion coming from upstairs. Adolphe said that he and a friend, Simon Kruger, went up to ask just what William was playing at. On knocking on the door they were met by a slightly fatigued Mr Staples, who appeared somewhat out of breath. To the picture dealer it seemed obvious that he had been jumping about causing the trouble.

James Yapp, the shop boy, gave corroborative evidence and David Francis, a joiner, gave evidence as to the cost of the damage.

For the defence Mr Anderson called Thomas Jones of Whitefield Road, Everton. He was a car proprietor who attested that on 11 January he had visited Mr Staple's other studio in Canning Place, Liverpool, to have his

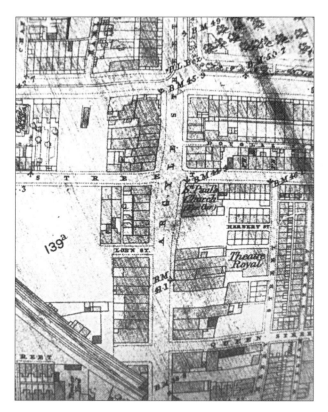

*Argyle Street, shown on a map
from the late nineteenth century.*

photograph taken for his birthday. Mr Jones stated that he was with
Mr Staples from ten-thirty to eleven-thirty and then again at twelve-thirty.
This in short proved a complete alibi for William Staples, who considered
himself completely guilt-free.

Mr Moore then began a second summons. It was for further alleged
jumping on the 19th, but for lesser damages amounting to £1 27s 6d.
Mr Koenigsberger claimed that in this instance, after another almighty
clamour caused by the jumping, William came downstairs and walked past
his door several times looking very pleased with himself. 'You'll have to pay
the damage!' bawled Adolphe.

'Go along with you, you bloody German,' William was alleged to have
retorted, before poking his tongue out and spreading his fingers over his
nose.

Mr Anderson said that there was no jumping whatsoever, only the moving
of scenery about as required for customers of a photography studio. His client
was the one who was constantly being insulted, and Mrs Staples had also
been threatened. He called to the stand George Williams, a scenery painter,

who said that he was with the defendant in Liverpool up until one-thirty on the day in question.

Mr Preston was no fool and he had no doubt that the damage described had been caused by jumping. In the first summons, it was clear from the evidence that Mr Jones gave that William was in Liverpool at the time of the alleged offence, so it could not possibly have been him. And for the second, although it had been proved the defendant was in his studio at some point that day, the magistrate failed to be satisfied beyond reasonable doubt that the defendant had actually jumped or at least not to cause damage intentionally. He therefore had no choice but to dismiss the case.

'If you are in fact guilty of this crime Mr Staples, then it was one of the meanest, dirtiest and spiteful things one man could do to another,' said Mr Preston. With this warning, William was free to go.

THE LADY OF THE LAKE

On the night of 2 April 1904, Alfred Lee left his lodgings at 61 Mount Pleasant, Liverpool, and made the short walk down to see his wife Frances, who was waiting longingly for her escort to James Street station. She was an assistant at a tobacconist shop in Preesons Row and in her grasp she clutched a pretty bouquet of flowers for her mother. The pair had married only weeks before, but Alfred had recently lost his job, forcing the couple to temporarily live apart until he could find a suitable situation. He was soon in the arms of his beloved spouse and at about nine o'clock they took the train to Hamilton Square, then a tram from Claughton Road to Birkenhead Park. On arrival the couple walked hand-in-hand around the moonlit, tree-lined roads, picking extra daffodils for Frances' mother. As they neared the park gates in Ashville Road, the romantic scene faded and a marital tiff arose. Troublesome words were heatedly exchanged during which Alfred turned to cross the road. He had had a rather ill-timed call of nature and lined himself against a wall for some urgent relief. With Alfred's back turned, his furious eighteen-year-old bride took a firm hold of the large iron park gates and began to climb. Alfred turned his head and was more than a little surprised to see Frances making her way over the metallic structure, which was approximately 7ft in height. Mr Lee was so dumbstruck by the sight that he failed to restrain his wife from running off into the park, crying in hysterics.

'Dolly! Dolly!' he shouted after her. Alfred adjusted his trousers and headed for the gate. Once over he searched the park for more than an hour, but his beloved Frances had somehow disappeared without trace. Alfred retraced his steps and made his way to his father-in-law's house at 57 Park Road East. Wringing his hands with worry he fervently informed Mr John Barker of the alarming circumstances.

'Dolly! Dolly!' he cried breathlessly.

'What? What is it?' John urgently queried.

'Dolly is in the park!'

'What, now?' asked her perplexed parent.

'Yes, since ten o'clock. What shall I do?'

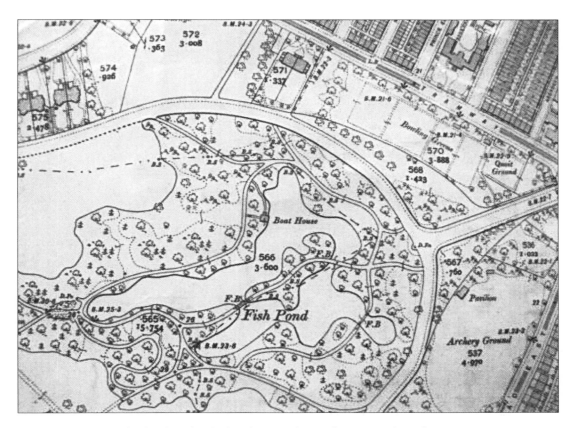

Birkenhead Park. The boathouse is featured prominently in the centre.

John quickly put on his coat and hurried with Alfred back to the park. The atmosphere was one of fear and anger. It had only been two months since Mr Barker had refused to his give his blessing to the couple's wedding, but due to some unforeseen circumstances he had been forced to relent. The gate was too high for the middle-aged Mr Barker to negotiate so he went off to find an alternative route. There was none. In the meantime Alfred went back to the house in Park Road East to see if his spouse had returned. He was met by Mrs Barker, who brokenly sobbed that Frances had not yet come back, and that he should get off her property and go find her.

'I will make you find her,' fumed Mr Barker, bearing an undeniable look of hate upon catching sight of the returning Mr Lee.

Alfred soon scrambled over the gate and tried again to find his missing wife. After a lengthy search with still no luck, Mr Barker decided it would be best to contact the police and reluctantly reported his daughter as officially missing. Alfred Lee went home to Liverpool in a cab. Perhaps she had gone there.

The imposing park gates seen in Ashville Road.

Inspector Stockton was sent to meet Mr Barker at the police station, where he gave a statement. The inspector telephoned his colleagues in Liverpool and requested that Mr Lee be brought back to Birkenhead without delay.

It was Detective William Whiteside's job to go and fetch the man from his hotel at Mount Pleasant. He only knew that a woman was missing and was oblivious to the exact need for Mr Lee to be taken to Wirral. He gave a knock on the door and in a raised voice was told that it was open. Alfred was sitting on the bed in his shirt and pants, lost deep in thought. 'I need you to come to Birkenhead to look for a missing lady,' said the detective.

'You mean my wife? Has she been found?', asked Mr Lee, as he raised his head. 'I am very glad you came. I was expecting a detective to come. I will go across with you to Birkenhead and give them all the information I can.'

The detective cautioned Mr Lee as to what he was saying as it might be used against him. 'Poor Dolly,' Lee mused, 'she'll be found in the pond.'

Detective Whiteside escorted Lee to the landing stage and they boarded a ferry over the river. The officer told the stageman to make a note of Mr Lee's departure and informed him that he would be bringing the man back later on. During the journey Alfred remarked again that he supposed Frances would be found in the park's pond. A rendezvous was arranged at the park entrance for about three o'clock that morning and, privately, the detective spoke to Inspector Stockton and told him of Mr Lee's ominous comments. Alfred was asked whether he could offer any further information about the whereabouts of his runaway wife. 'I would first like to know whether I am in custody or not,' he enquired.

'No, Mr Lee, you are not,' answered the inspector.

Alfred then went on to relate his version of the night's proceedings. He said that his wife had left him at the gates in Ashville Road and had climbed over into the park. The officer went over to the gates in question and shone his lantern. There were no marks on them whatsoever and this suspicious fact was pointed out to Lee.

'Let's go to the other gates, higher up,' he replied. The men headed over to a second set of gates and these were checked over by the inspector.

'Oh heaven! They are the flowers she brought from Liverpool! These are the gates she got over,' exclaimed Alfred, as he pointed towards a sombre set of flowers stuck high upon the railings. There were two or three of the same strewn on the ground that had evidently fallen during Mrs Lee's climb. Inspector Stockton found several marks where paint had been rubbed from the metal, with marks also distinguishable on the upper spikes. Mr Lee described how his wife had got over the gate and where he had seen her place her foot on the padlock. The entrance was opened and the officer and Mr Lee commenced searching for the missing woman. It was not long before Mr Barker blew a whistle alerting the two to his finding. He had gone to search on his own and had discovered his daughter's red tam-a-shanter hat near to the boathouse. The three went to the spot where the item was found and could find no trace of any disturbance or irregularities. Alfred was clearly becoming agitated and it was decided that it would be wise to have him taken to the Price Street police station for questioning, but first Stockton ordered for grappling irons to be brought to the park for a search of the lake. At about a quarter-to-eight in the morning, once darkness had faded, the watery depths were investigated and the mackintosh-clad body of Frances Lee was discovered. It lay submerged about fifteen yards from the boathouse

The boathouse in Birkenhead Park. Frances' body was pulled from these very waters.

in approximately 10ft of water, and the cadaver was taken to the mortuary for specialists to examine later that week. Several inquest sittings concerning the unusual death commenced on the subsequent Tuesday.

The first witness to be called was PC Thomas Evans. He had been on duty in the neighbourhood of the park on the day in question and it was he who had locked the gates. 'I have no doubt all the gates were locked,' said the constable.

Lillian Baker of Lloyd Street, Liverpool deposed that she was the deceased's employer at the tobacconist store in Preesons Row. She addressed the deceased as Miss Lee and said that in April she had been told that Frances had been engaged to be married, but the ceremony was called off.

'Did she say why?' enquired the coroner.

'Because the young man had been embezzling money,' answered Mrs Baker. She continued her statement, saying that on 2 April, at about one forty-five, the deceased left for her lunch break after working well all morning. In the afternoon her father came into the shop, joined by Mr Lee. Frances said that Mr Lee was a relation of hers. Frances left at about six and returned at seven, and at about nine o'clock the pair left together seemingly on friendly terms.

The Revd David Caldarin, a Persian priest, was next to be called. He lodged in the same property as Mr Lee. The holy man attested that on the evening in question he met with Alfred and was introduced to the deceased, as his wife. 'She invited me in for some tea with them,' said the reverend. He told her that he was sorry but could not accept the invitation as he was expecting his supper soon. 'The woman had a cup of tea but she did not finish it. I asked her why. She answered that she had to get back to her work at the shop when Mr Lee rudely interrupted. The prisoner then said, "don't be an ass,"' deposed the reverend. 'Frances apologised on his behalf. He immediately added that he was sorry and really did not mean anything by it,' witness added.

The court heard how Mr Lee had called the marriage unfortunate. The reverend told him to have courage and reminded him that he had only been married for six weeks. 'She has been working for you and you have no children. You must not lose courage.'

'Yes but it is so hard,' Lee sighed.

A modern-day view of the boathouse.

The young woman confided in the priest that she did her best to cheer him up. 'She was in the best of spirits all that time, jolly and never seemed depressed,' Revd Caldarin recounted. It was heard that Mrs Lee was always trying to cheer up her desolate husband but he always acted morose. She had asked her husband to talk with the witness, remarking that a clergyman such as himself would provide good counsel. Revd Caldarin concluded that after a few more minutes of conversation, the pair left apparently on good terms.

'After several conversations with Mr Lee, you formed the opinion that he was very fond of the deceased?' questioned defence solicitor Mr Smith.

'Oh yes. I didn't see anything otherwise than that they loved each other. His depression or despondency was because he was just married but could not live with his wife. He was anxious as an honourable man to earn money to maintain his wife.'

William Massey, an electric car conductor, next took to the stand. He deposed that at around nine-thirty on the night of the death his car left Woodside to Hamilton Square. The prisoner and the deceased climbed on board. 'The young woman had some yellow flowers and wore a mackintosh and a red tam-a-shanter hat. The man wore a dark blue suit and I noticed his felt hat in his hand,' said the conductor. As far as he could see they were on friendly terms.

An alternative view came from Eileen Cookson, a blacksmith's wife from Paterson Street. She stated that she was on her way to Grange Road at approximately nine-thirty and on arriving at a small passage leading to Craven Street, she saw two people arguing. 'The man pushed the woman towards the wall and she screamed. He had something in his hand like a coat and said, "take this." The woman said, "no, I won't."' He threw the coat to her and she ran out of the entry across Paterson Street and up the passage that led to Park Road East. The man ran after her calling her a foul name. 'I went to see what was going on but I could not find them,' she recounted.

'Can you identify the man? Is there anybody here like him?' asked Coroner Holden. Mrs Cookson scanned the room and her eyes soon settled on the prisoner. 'Well, I believe that looks like the man,' she replied with an accusatory gesture of the hand.

'Are you prepared to swear he is the man?'

Eileen paused for a moment. 'I am not prepared to swear, but he is very like the man I saw.'

The woman the witness saw was described as wearing a blue blouse and dark skirt with a very flat hat. Mrs Cookson said that she had not seen anything in the papers in regards to Mrs Lee's attire. In fact, Eileen Cookson could not read at all.

'The man she saw had on a cap. All she was really sure about was that there was a man and a woman quarrelling,' interjected Frederick Smith, his voice toned with legal strategy.

Mr John William Barker was asked to give evidence and he was soon to disclose some sensational facts. Since October last he had resided in Park Road East. Before then he had resided in Waterloo. He knew that Alfred had been paying special attention to his daughter and in the early part of December John had received a surprise visit from him. 'He came to ask for Frances' hand in marriage,' said John, fighting back emotion. He told the court that he had no objection to the marriage, as long as Mr Lee was a person of respectability. By January Mr Barker confessed that he had changed his mind and audibly declared that Alfred was not a suitable match. The news was not taken well by his daughter and she vowed to be with her love no matter what. The court was told that on the evening of the 12th, the deceased and the prisoner went to Waterloo with the idea of seeing Alfred's mother. On the following morning, Mr Barker received a chilling letter, penned by his daughter's own hand:

I hope you will forgive me for what I have done. I have taken the laudanum much against Alf's wishes. I have done this because I could not live without Alf. We wish you to hurry us together. Be brave, and think of us as kindly as you can. We are sorry to give you such a lot of trouble, but it is for the best. Goodbye my dear parents, trusting God will forgive us.
Affectionately yours,
Dolly

As if that wasn't enough, on the rear was written a second heart-wrenching note:

Do not attempt to stop the effects as we will do the same thing again. Let us die in peace.
Dolly

Underneath, the prisoner had also written a short message of his own:

You will understand that although we are in bed together there is no sin in doing so. Surely you will understand that we cannot go in front of our Maker with that upon our souls. Please forgive us.

Mr Barker said upon reading the letter he travelled to Liverpool in search of his daughter and had reported the matter to the police. He searched until 15 February, when he met her walking around Islington. After a dramatic reunion Miss Barker took her father to the house where she and Alfred were staying. John begrudgingly invited his daughter and Mr Lee back to his home in Birkenhead. At least there he could keep an eye on them.

On 25 February, Mr Barker said that he had taken them to the Registrar's Office. They were married in his presence, albeit under stressful circumstances. The couple lived happily together at Park Road East until 28 March, when the witness requested that his new son-in-law pack up and leave. He was still jobless and was becoming something of an expensive and unwanted burden. Frances would often stay at his new residence at Mount Pleasant, but always seemed low spirited when at home in the evenings.

'I last saw her alive on 2 April at about four o'clock at the Ship Inn in Preesons Row,' said Mr Barker. 'She seemed quite happy and jolly.'

Coroner Holden cleared his throat. 'Your daughter was a very strong, healthy girl?'

'I should have thought she was, although I do not think she excelled in being active.'

'She was rather impetuous at times, was she not?' probed Mr Smith.

'No, no I don't think so. She had a level head.'

Mr Smith held up an envelope. 'Have you seen this letter she sent to Lee?'

The man's brow declined slightly and he shook his head.

'Dear Alf, please forget all about last night. My temper and passion always gets in the way. That such a thing should happen is really awful,' Smith quoted.

Mr Barker said that he had never seen the letter before in his life.

'Before the laudanum incident, had you any trouble of that kind with your daughter?'

'No sir.'

'And at that time you found that Lee was in some kind of financial trouble?'

'Yes.'

Mrs Barker was next to speak. She was draped in shades of deep black and was helped into a chair by courteous court aids. The woman gave evidence to the effect that in February she thought that her daughter had gone out to visit Mrs Lee in Waterloo. The next day, however, she had received the horrifying letter which had just been read out. On reuniting with Frances, Mrs Barker begged to know why she had attempted the poisonous suicide bid.

'She told me it was because of monetary difficulties.' She added that Frances had admitted that it was Lee who had brought the poison and that they both suffered awfully from its effects. 'On Saturday she left home for the last time. She was wearing a pale blue blouse, a brown mackintosh and a tam-a-shanter.' Clearly grieving, Mrs Barker told Mr Holden that Frances had told her of a previous attempt to end her life.

'Oh they tried twice?' was the coroner's surprised reply.

'Yes, the second time was in Norton Street, Liverpool.'

Mr Smith skilfully summed up the facts of her evidence.

'It was momentary difficulties that made Lee attempt it, but he got over the trouble soon afterwards. The young people were constantly together after Lee left Park Road East and they were evidently anxious to be together. Going through the park was one of their frequent walks.'

'Did she happen to tell you how they got in there after dark?' asked Mr Holden.

Mrs Barker wiped away a tear. 'She said they knew of a private way.'

An employee from Woodside Ferry spoke of how he witnessed a young man matching Alfred Lee's description walking about the landing stage just after half-twelve on the night of 2 April. 'He asked me what time the next boat was and I said about twelve-forty. When I replied he said, "twenty to one, you remember that." I thought that was a little strange and I looked at him as he walked off smoking a cigarette.'

'Did you think he was sober?' asked Mr Holden.

'I was inclined to think he had had a drop to drink.'

A cab driver by the name of Edward Packyngham deposed that on the Sunday morning of 3 April, at about one o'clock, Mr Lee hailed his vehicle and got in at St George's landing stage. The cab window somehow became broken and Mr Lee caused a dispute, during which a policeman had to be called. The court heard how the prisoner willingly gave his name and address and afterwards paid his fare, plus something for the shattered window. 'He looked flurried and dazed, but seemed quite sober,' said the driver.

Further evidence was heard from Thomas Harris of the Temperance Hotel, 61 Mount Pleasant. He recalled seeing Lee come in at one o'clock and later seeing him leave with another man about twenty minutes afterwards. The man was Detective Whiteside.

A park keeper stated that on one afternoon Alfred had asked him about the depth of the water by the boathouse. 'He asked if a man could "dive off there without touching the bottom". I had seen Lee sitting in there on several occasions.'

'Mr Holden the park keeper is always being asked about the depth of the water,' said Mr Smith, standing at his desk in readiness, before sitting down just as fast.

Mrs Stewart of 41 Norton Street recalled the deceased and the prisoner staying at her property one evening in February. Next morning they were both ill, but recovered and left.

'This was the occasion they took the poison?' Mr Holden enquired.

'Oh I don't know anything about that,' she gushed.

The court also heard evidence from Inspector Stockton, Detective Whiteside and Chief Constable Davies. Sergeant Johnson, who escorted Mr Lee to Walton between inquest sittings, recalled that the prisoner had remarked to him that he was a good swimmer and referred to his performances in Malta. The sergeant added that he was present when a letter was found upon the prisoner.

'Another letter?' queried the coroner.

The officer read it aloud to the densely packed chamber:

I am not very strong. My heart is weak and may give way under tonight's strain. If my darling is alive I am satisfied. If not, of course I shall go to her. I think God has spared her for me and answered my prayers.

Dr Preece, the police surgeon, attested to making the post-mortem upon the body of Frances Lee. He said that he could find no marks of violence upon the corpse and it was in such a state as to lead him to believe death was due to drowning. In his professional opinion the cause of death was asphyxia, consequent upon immersion in water. She was not pregnant.

Coroner Holden declared that there was no doubt that the deceased died from drowning, but it was up to the jury to decide how Frances got into the water. He added that the statement Lee made to Detective Whiteside might be taken by some as an admission of guilt, but any man with common sense knew that his position was one of grave suspicion. 'He would have overstepped the mark to say that he was exceedingly astonished to find that the police wanted him at all. No doubt there were the circumstances that he said, "she'll be found in the park," but you must remember that the prisoner knew that his wife had already made two attempts to take her life.'

The jury took this into consideration and retired to consult upon a verdict. After a relatively short deliberation, they returned with an indecisive open verdict. This of course meant relatively little unless agreed with by the fate-wielding borough magistrates.

The funeral of Frances Dolores Lee took place at noon on 7 April at Flaybrick Hill cemetery. Her weeping relatives wished the occasion to be a quiet affair and arranged for an interment at the most inconvenient time for overly-keen members of the public. However, at half-past ten on the morning of the service, Park Road East became swamped with spectators who had congregated along the roadside. Many mourners held daffodils as a sign of respect. Although some showed genuine grief, many wished only to catch a glimpse of the accused, who it was rumoured may put in an appearance. Frances was once heard to remark that if anything ever did happen to her she wished her funeral to feature bay horses rather than depressing black ones, and her wish was granted. The coffin was of polished oak with neat brass fittings. As the cortége moved off to Mrs Lee's final resting place, the several hundred mourners all bowed their heads in silence. On entering the cemetery constables cordoned off the freshly dug grave with rope and a posse of police stood firmly on guard. The funeral was, of course, full of sorrow but thankfully passed without issue.

On Tuesday 19 April, Alfred was forced to face magistrates on a charge of wilful murder. The three learned men took their seats and almost immediately the prisoner was called for: 'Put up Alfred Harris Lee.' He stepped up to the dock in one swift step with a calm air, probably acquired during his army days. He was a handsome young man of medium height and wore a moustache. He looked physically powerful, but his stance was one of quiet reserve. Alfred had attired himself in a dark navy, almost black suit with a black band of the same around his hat.

The magistrates were informed of the outcome of the very thorough proceedings of the inquest and were told that no new evidence had become available. There was no firm evidence to show guilt on the part of Mr Lee and it was requested that he be discharged. After a moment of hushed suspense a final decision was made.

'Lee, as there is no evidence against you, you are discharged.'

On hearing the announcement Alfred blushed with long-awaited relief. He turned fast and looked to the spectators in the stalls. Many had anticipated such an outcome and cheered with support. Frederick Smith and members of the press rushed out to the front entrance into the expectant gaze of curious crowds. Mr Lee, however, escaped this public scrutiny and made a quick departure through another door. However, he could never escape the memories of the dreadful affair in which he had found himself. Those thoughts would continue to haunt him for the rest of his days.

BEATEN BOBBIES

PC Taylor was on duty on the night of Saturday 4 October 1913, his beat taking him towards Birkenhead's Bentinck Street. News of trouble brewing in the area had been put to him and the constable walked briskly to the scene of the alleged disturbance. On turning into the street he came across a gang of youths engaged in a thuggish adolescent stand-off. Four or five of the young men were stood with their backs pressed against the wall. They seemed to be antagonising someone in the crowd opposite to come and fight. Their faces were swollen with a dark rainbow of colours and grazed with many cuts and scratches.

PC Taylor walked up to them and asked what was going on. 'We're waiting for a row,' replied one of the youths proudly. The constable looked on without a flinch. 'I think you should all get home,' he told them. They refused.

Constable Taylor was not afraid of instilling a bit of due discipline and took hold of the lads by their collars. He tried to forcibly start them off on their exit but the plan backfired as some of the gang formed a tight circle around the officer, hurling insults at him nose to nose. The houses of Laxey Terrace sat some 15ft down from the pavement of Bentinck Street, and it was there that Constable Taylor was almost sent flying. He was knocked to the ground with a hard punch to the jaw. A small gathering of passer-bys and one or two members of the crowd who disagreed with the outrage launched a bid to save the officer. The shrill cry of a whistle shot through the air as PC Taylor was kicked in the face and about his abdomen. PC Humphries ran over with PC Williams; the latter was off duty and had heard the plea for help from his nearby home. Both grappled with the thugs and in their efforts received several blows themselves. The crowd of men fell to the ground in a bloodied heap. Some of the gang accidentally kicked two of their own. Brothers Samuel and Thomas Stanley were struck hard. Samuel ran away in pain whilst Thomas pretended to be unconscious as he realised the police were gaining the upper hand. The gang scattered, leaving Thomas alone at the roadside to face the full force of the law. His acting skills left a lot to be desired and as soon as a cup of water was poured over the 'unconscious'

Above: *Bentinck Street, as shown in 2009.*

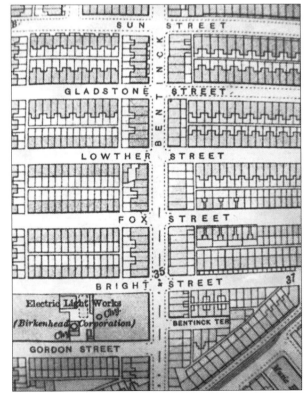

Right: *Bentinck Street on a map from the early twentieth century.*

youth, he came to life amidst a string of profanities. The rather wet Mr Stanley was raised to his feet and shackled with a heavy set of handcuffs. It was during this imprisonment that Constable Williams was unexpectedly struck from behind, momentarily stunning him. The prisoner's brother had returned and it was up to PC Bushell to chase the sibling down the street. He pursued him into Brassey Street, where an observant member of the public successfully delivered a trip. The fugitive landed flat on his face, thus allowing the officer to make his much-deserved arrest.

By the end of the twenty-minute episode of chaos, PC Taylor had been dealt some serious bruising, PC Williams had suffered a kick to the head and a blow to his eye, and Constable Humphries complained of a painful arm and leg, along with a blackened chin. All the officers' clothes were torn and their helmets completely smashed in.

Samuel and Thomas Stanley, of Vulcan Street, stood before magistrates the following Monday charged with being drunk and disorderly and with assaulting PCs Taylor and Humphries. The prisoners were each sent to gaol for three months for assaulting PC Taylor and three months for the attack on his colleague. The sentences ran consecutively.

MADNESS AT HOYLAKE

Considerable commotion was created amongst the otherwise docile passengers of the 6.50 train to Hoylake one evening, as it arrived at its destination on 11 January 1909. As the steaming locomotive chugged to a halt at the platform, a rather excitable ticket holder by the name of Edward Armitage popped his head out the door and stepped down from his carriage. He had been to town and had evidently enjoyed one or two more glasses of wine than he should have. His giddy voice hollered throughout the station

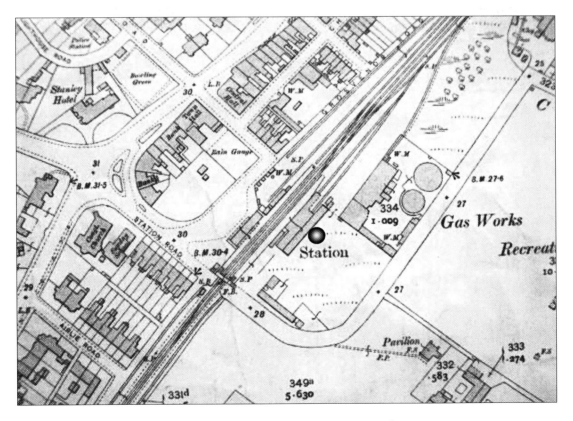

Hoylake station on a map from the early twentieth century.

Hoylake railway station, as seen in the early twentieth century.

Hoylake station entrance, 2009.

and he began to talk loudly and gesticulate in an extraordinary manner. He eventually calmed down and rested himself upon the bags of a luggage truck. The porter pushing the truck asked if Edward minded getting off, but this was simply laughed off.

Station master Cherry was made aware of the bother but even he could not persuade the drunken man to budge from the barrow. The station master's threats of police action were equally unheeded, so Sergeant Finchett was summoned in a further attempt to remove the nuisance. For about ten minutes the officer talked to Armitage and in the end managed to convince him to go home. Sergeant Finchett physically helped the man off the cart and walked with him to the railway station forecourt. A cab was hailed and the horse soon pulled up with a frosty neigh. The sergeant politely opened the carriage door for Mr Armitage, expecting him to hop in and take a seat. Armitage however, had other, more dangerous plans. No sooner had he entered the carriage by one door than he exited it by the other. He then scrambled to the ground and crawled underneath the carriage. 'Get on with it horse!' he shouted crazily. The driver was about to order the go ahead but luckily realised the situation. He promptly grabbed the reigns at the horse's head and gave a hard tug backwards. By now a crowd of onlookers had amassed to see what all the fuss was about. They watched in curiosity as Edward raised himself from the ground and pushed aside Sergeant Finchett and the porters as if they were children. He ran towards the crossing gate and scaled it like a monkey. Pursuers failed to catch up with the man who had outrun them down the line towards West Kirby, but Edward was quickly located with his head resting upon the rail. 'Come and cut my head off!' he screamed. Sergeant Finchett's patience had all but gone and he ordered reinforcements to apprehend Edward and take him to the Prussia Street police station.

The next morning he was brought to stand trial for his disruptive behaviour. To magistrates he professed his most sincere apologies, but it was too little too late. As well as a severe admonishment, Edward was ordered to pay 20s and courts costs for his disgraceful folly.

MUSICAL INDECENCY

Richard Oliver was a twenty-six-year-old teacher who had taught many young aspiring musicians across the Wirral. In the month of March 1884, Richard was approached by the Simpson family who wished him to tutor their daughter. Fanny Simpson was only seven years of age but was a keen little girl whose only ambition was to play the piano. She had previously been taught by a female tutor and had enjoyed learning the *Elfin Waltz*, at which she was quite proficient. It was arranged that Mr Oliver would call at the house, 59 Marion Street, twice a week and teach the girl to play.

By June of that year Mr and Mrs Simpson had begun to doubt the arrangement. It was not uncommon to hear Fanny getting upset during the lessons, but until now her parents had not suspected anything improper was afoot. The child had been making good progress with her learning but she now made some very serious allegations against her teacher, which sent Mrs Simpson into a frenzy. She was ready to kill Mr Oliver for his alleged indecency against her little girl at the first opportunity, but her husband persuaded her different. He was equally enraged, but devised a more cunning plan to try and catch the fiend in the act. John Lemon, a plumber and friend of the family was contacted and he made his way around to the house later that afternoon. Mr Oliver was due later that evening.

It was devised that he and Mr Simpson would hide away and communicate by means of a length of cotton. If anything unsavoury was seen to occur, then they would secretly signal to each other and make a joint ambush. The father hid himself away under the sofa and clutched an almost invisible piece of cotton tightly between his forefinger and thumb. This trail led to a small room under the stairs, in which Mr Lemon stood silently.

It wasn't long before Mr Oliver arrived at the house, prompt and on time as usual. Mrs Simpson headed to the door and amazingly managed to hold her tongue. 'Good evening, Mr Oliver,' she said with a false smile. 'Come through.'

She led the teacher into the back room and offered him a seat.

'Thank you Mrs Simpson, you are most kind.'

'Fanny will be down in a moment.'

The remaining portion of Marion Street.

Mr Oliver nodded politely, hands clasped over his knee, legs crossed, and waited. He was completely oblivious to Mr Simpson hiding in the room, watching keenly, only a matter of feet away.

The gentle patter of Fanny's innocent feet resounded through the hallway. Only a few minutes had passed before the girl's father saw something peculiar, but nevertheless bided his time, giving only a gentle tug on the string as a warning. A quarter of an hour later the teacher's conduct became so untoward that Mr Simpson gave the signal. John Lemon came bursting into the room. Seconds later Mr Simpson scrambled out from under the sofa, venting his outrage.

'What are you doing with my child in that position?' he demanded.

Mr Oliver became flustered and made his excuses to leave. It was Mrs Simpson who blocked his path and she commenced to hit him, swinging a bag of onions down upon the man's head. He was going nowhere.

Detective Moore was called to the house and he arrested the musician on a charge of indecent assault. Mr Oliver indignantly denied any wrongdoing and gave his reasons for his apparent impropriety. He explained that the girl was of a temperamental nature, which occasionally required him to hold her round the waist in order to achieve concentration.

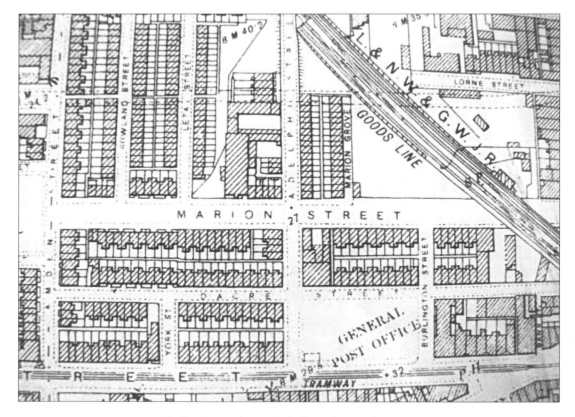

Marion Street shown in the late nineteenth century.

In the courtroom George Morton, father to another of Richard's scholars, spoke in his defence. His daughter had been under the guidance of Mr Oliver for fifteen months and considered him to be a thoroughly sober and religious man whom he could trust with any of his children.

'Are you prepared to trust him after hearing this case?' inquired Recorder Clement Higgins.

'I am.'

Mr McGaw, a joiner and builder, gave a similar complimentary testimony, stating that the accused had taught his daughter for eighteen months and that he believed his behaviour to be impeccable.

After considerable deliberation the jury found the once reputable teacher guilty, but recommended him to mercy. Richard Oliver was then sent to prison for four months with hard labour. It is hoped Mr Oliver reviewed his controversial teaching methods on his eventual release.

WHAT THE BUTLER DID

At the County Court on Tuesday 10 August 1869, Frederick Welmin formally sued his employer, Edward Logan, for the sum of £1 17s 6d, a balance of wages alleged to be overdue. Frederick had been butler to Mr Logan, who resided at the awe-inspiring Thurstaston Hall. He claimed that his annual pay was £50 a year but he had left on 26 June and had not been paid a month's wages in lieu of his notice. Judge Harden listened to testimony from Mr Logan who disclosed some of the plaintiff's particularly embarrassing actions.

It was explained that on the evening of 8 June Edward had held a dinner party at his palatial country pad for some of his closest friends and acquaintances. Welmin was scheduled to be on duty and was expected to exhibit the utmost professionalism, particularly when entertaining

The stately Thurstaston Hall.

The unchanged façade of Thursaton Hall today.

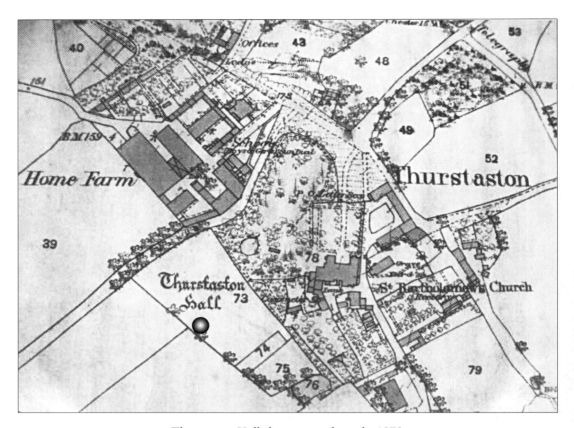

Thurstaston Hall, from a map from the 1870s.

guests. Contrary to his employer's belief the butler chose to become rather intoxicated and, according to the host, acted somewhat appallingly. In fact, Welmin's inebriation was such that he could not distinguish one dish from another. A gentleman asked for beef, but was abruptly handed a plate of jelly. On requesting jelly, he was given beef! Mr Logan remonstrated with his servant and quietly asked him to make his exit for the night. But the jovial butler would not listen and refused point blank. He drunkenly spoke to the guests as if he was one himself, amusing some but annoying others. Edward had run out of ideas; a servant had never behaved in this way before and Welmin seemed to have no intention of shutting up. As a last resort Mr Logan proposed that he and his friends should adjourn early to the drawing room, leaving the butler alone at the table. The evening carried on pleasantly enough, but the general mood of the party had been spoilt.

The following morning Edward called Frederick into his dressing room for a talk. He commenced to describe the previous night's events and expressed his deep disappointment. Welmin pretended to be oblivious to the events and was discharged. The court heard how Frederick then told of his sorrow and regret and how he wished his master to reconsider. He pleaded for a week or so to stay and redeem himself from his incredulous manner, but Logan's decision was final. In the spirit of generosity he allowed Welmin to remain at the house until the 26th; plenty of time to sort himself out. The plaintiff happily agreed to these conditions and on the 26th settled his accounts. Edward paid him £3 16s, a sum that Fredrick at the time seemed happy with.

His Honour was of the view that the claim now was one of a most selfish nature. The defendant had treated the plaintiff beyond the call of normal kindness. In March Welmin sprained his ankle whilst at work and on hearing of the accident Mr Logan contacted Dr Russell and paid the medical bill of 3s 6d from his own pocket. It was Judge Harden's opinion that the former butler was now pushing his luck and certainly trying to take advantage. The case was immediately thrown out.

TREASURE IN THE SAND HILLS

On the afternoon 6 June 1917, Headmaster Arthur Grounds, of the Hoylake Higher Elementary School, opened the small private cupboard next to his desk. Inside he placed a small parcel containing a total of £7 19s 6d believing it to be a safe financial haven. The following morning Mr Grounds arrived to start work, but on searching his cupboard found that the cash had vanished. It later became apparent that student Kathleen Grier was also missing a pricey fountain pen that she had left in her flip-top wooden desk before heading home the previous day. School staff were informed of the worrying incidents and an investigation was launched. It was not long before the caretaker discovered that a single window had been left unfastened overnight. Whoever committed the robberies must have gained access to the property via this opportune route. PC Francis was ordered to the school to take statements and to try and get to the bottom of this academic atrocity. He learnt that a nine-year-old boy had information regarding the thefts; he had actually played a part in them. The lad took the officer to the nearby sand hills and showed him where he and two other boys had hidden £3 of the missing money. Constable Francis was also told that his joy-seeking

Hoylake Elementary School depicted in 1917.

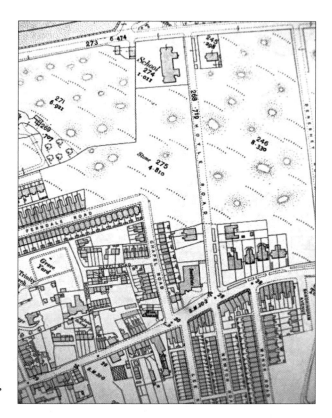

Hoylake, the scene of the theft, shown in 1912.

accomplices had more than likely gone off to spend their booty at that fairs in New Brighton. It was there that they were later traced and found to be spending the money without a tinge of guilt. They were immediately charged with theft.

On Monday 11 June the three lads faced magistrates. The defence solicitor deposed that one of the boys on trial, a ten-year-old, was one of seven children and all but he were a credit to his parents. Despite numerous whippings and fines the boy would not relent and his mother and father now requested he be sent away. The eldest scamp had also been birched on several occasions for previous thefts, but he too had failed to give up his youthful criminality. The youngest had never been in any trouble and came from a loving family and a splendid home. It was supposed that his so-called friends led him astray and he was looked upon more leniently. He was discharged with a caution whilst the older pair were sent to the reformatory in a further attempt to correct their wayward behaviour.

THE PRENTON LANE MANIAC

In Woodchurch's Prenton Lane there once stood three small cottages. Within one of the dwellings lived forty-eight-year-old widower Mrs Elizabeth Thomas and her three sons. There was the first-born William, aged twenty-five; Joseph, aged twenty-three; and Samuel, who was the youngest of the trio, aged only nine.

The Saturday night of 31 July 1851 saw Elizabeth and Samuel patiently waiting up for the return of the two brothers, who had gone out for a summer night's stroll. At about nine o'clock William returned alone.

'What are you both still up for?' he asked sharply.

'We were waiting for you and Joseph to come home,' his mother replied, a little shocked at his aggressive tone. She was well aware that William had had some trouble of mind lately but hoped it would soon pass. Sometimes he suffered from headaches so bad that he had been forced to stay home from work, and help from doctors seemed only to alleviate the symptoms temporarily.

'Never mind. I will sit for Joe,' said William. 'You go to bed. I'll wait.'

Elizabeth supposed there was no real need for them all to stay up so she said goodnight and ushered Samuel up the stairs and into her bed, where he usually slept. William waited until they were safely out of earshot and headed for the garden. It was beginning to get dark. He grabbed a sturdy spade and struck hard into the grassy turf, digging up mounds of earth until he had dug a hole of some considerable depth. With that done William went back inside the cottage and lit a candle, and from a cabinet he retrieved a razor. It was cut-throat sharp. The young man crept up the stairs, blade in one hand, candle in the other, and proceeded towards his mothers' bedroom.

Five minutes later little Samuel was awoken by a series of rough kicks and subdued moans from his mother. He opened his weary eyes and was shaken to discover the silhouette of his brother kneeling on top of their mum. The boy let out a shrill shriek.

'Shhhhh!' urged William. He set the candle down on the window sill and grabbed Elizabeth's throat, slicing it open with the blade. She struggled, but the speed of William's actions coupled with the shock of the whole affair rendered her body dumb with abject terror. A few seconds of resistance passed before Mrs Thomas's body relinquished into the stillness of death. Samuel's cries echoed about the whole house. A bloodstained William got off the bed and hurried around to his brother's side of the bed. 'Shhhhh,' he repeated, as he lifted Samuel off the bed and carried the frightened child to his own room at the front of the house, where he laid him on the bed. 'I'll be with you now,' he added and he gave the boy two kisses. William put on some clean clothes then left the room to return to the crime scene. He bound the decreasingly warm hands of his mother tight with a handkerchief and rolled her up in the crimson bedspread. He tied a rope around the woman's waist and dragged her from the bedroom, along the darkened hallway and down the stairs. On hearing the noise Samuel crept out of bed to see what was happening. He watched the body being taken down the staircase; the neck and head lying limply from a gap in the bed sheets, thumping hard on each stair. William dragged the cadaver through the kitchen and out through the back gate. It was with some difficulty that he managed to heave the corpse up some stone steps leading to the garden, but he did it. The body was then lowered into the makeshift grave and buried with about 2ft of compost. William wiped his hands clean of mud with a sense of accomplishment and walked back into the house and up into the murder room. By now it was twenty to eleven and Joseph was just returning home from his evening out. He tried to quietly close the front door but it still made a noisy racket. 'Who's there?' William called out with a start.

'Me,' Joseph whispered, conscious not to wake his mother or Samuel; little did he know of the dreadful circumstances that had befallen his household. He would wake no one.

The middle son saw his older brother descend the staircase with a cold smile. 'Joe, I've killed mother and buried her in the garden. I've made her comfortable and she will be a good deal better off. Don't you go and say anything.'

Joseph broke down in a flood of tears. There was no doubt that William was capable of such a thing and his behaviour had been somewhat unusual of late. His dirty attire confirmed the deed.

Without a hint of guilt William guided his brother upstairs to see Samuel. Both brothers were now crying bitterly. 'What's the use of being that soft? She is better off,' remarked William callously. He seemed to hold no comprehension over the nature of his actions. As he wiped away his tears Joseph went over to Samuel, picked him up and carried the lad downstairs.

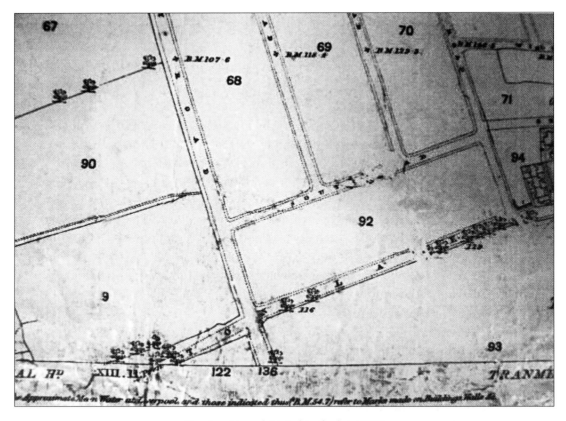

Prenton Lane depicted in the late 1800s.

'If you had been half an hour later it would have all been sided,' shouted William as they headed out the door.

Neighbour George Roydon was sound asleep when he was awoken by heavy knocking on his front door. The farmer went downstairs and discovered the two Thomas boys standing on his doorstep in obvious distress. He quickly invited them in and asked what on earth had happened. After hearing the sickening events he offered young Samuel a spare bed in the safety of his own cottage and agreed to return to the house to investigate. George put on his coat and followed Joseph into the back garden. From the glow of a candle they could see a patch of disturbed land with a recently-used spade lying nearby. Farmer Roydon dug down, removing a couple of feet of mud and finding the wrapped-up remains of Mrs Thomas lying below. Her heartbroken son fought hard to stem his tears and set off to inform the authorities.

PC Hughes arrived on the scene later that evening and arrested William Thomas for the crime of matricide. He recovered a pair of bloodstained trousers, a shirt and a flannel jacket from the house and took them back to the Bridewell as evidence.

The following week William was sent to stand trial before local magistrates and the charge was put to him.

'Guilty or not guilty?'

'No, I did not, not as I can recollect!' he answered with great vehemence. The man's demeanour in the dock fittingly reflected his tortured mindset, yet he seemed quite unconscious of the awful nature of his position.

Evidence from the two younger Thomas brothers was first heard and both accounts corroborated. Samuel said that William and his mother generally got on very well. 'She was always kind to him and he to her, except that sometimes he would "sauce" her a little. They had had no quarrel, but two or three days before I had heard him "sauce" her a little.'

The prisoner was asked whether he wished to ask Samuel any questions.

'Eh?' he answered loudly.

The question was repeated.

'No, I've nothing to ask him,' replied William in the same tone.

Joseph was called to the stand and spoke of his brother's recent erratic behaviour. 'There had been a difference in his manner for about a week before. He seemed to be getting gradually worse. Whenever I went in lately he ordered me out of the house.'

'Thou art a liar!' raged William. The unexpected outburst caused quite a sensation in the courtroom.

Joseph continued. 'He had been out of his mind previously and a surgeon attended him. He was never violent in his conduct but there had been something wrong about his head for nearly a year. I had often heard my mother alluding to the circumstance. He was never violent but for the last twelve months he seemed to be getting foolish and during the last week he became rather more excited.'

The views of George Roydon and PC Hughes were also taken into account. Testimony from surgeon Isaac Byerly was then put forth. He had known the family for some time, and it was he who had examined the gash across the deceased's neck.

'I know the prisoner who I have attended professionally,' began Isaac. 'Six or seven weeks ago his mother called me to see him. He complained of headache and drowsiness and betrayed other symptoms indicating an excited state of the brain. He was bled, and other appropriate remedies were used with a view to abating the excitement. He improved and at the end of the fortnight he told me that he felt quite well and was able to go back to work.

Two weeks ago however his mother came to me and said he had not been able to go to work and requested that I come and see him.' The medical man stated that he found William to be quite *compus mentus*, but Elizabeth disagreed, saying that her son had been making absurd remarks and being generally odd in his manner. 'I again ordered blistering and lowering remedies. On the day before the occurrence Mrs Thomas told me that he was not so well again, so I gave her a blister to be applied to the back of the neck and remarked that I would like to see him. I never saw her alive again.'

The court heard from Sir E. Cust. He had also spoken to the deceased the day before the murder regarding William's state of mind. 'On Friday morning I had some conversation with his mother and she said that if he became worse he should be removed to a lunatic asylum. William answered me quite rationally, and I thought his mental derangement was only temporary. His mother never complained to me of his using any violence, but only his absurd remarks.'

The evidence was clear. Elizabeth's death was undoubtedly caused by the manic actions of her eldest child. 'Do you have anything to say in answer to the charge?' enquired the magistrate. After a brief pause William replied, 'No, I have nothing to say.' He was sent to stand trial at the assizes.

Later that month William Thomas pleaded not guilty to the charge of wilful murder. This time he exhibited none of the aloofness he had displayed at his previous hearing, only occasionally frowning at various witnesses and casting expressive glances, as if taking a particular personal interest. No new evidence was submitted and after listening to the details heard at Birkenhead, the jury returned a verdict. They were satisfied that William Thomas was quite insane and should be acquitted for urgent medical treatment. The judge agreed and the prisoner was led away.

The quiet agricultural suburb of Woodchurch became awash with gossip and the tales of the Prenton Lane Maniac caused quite a sensation for many months to come.

A NOISY NEIGHBOUR

On 7 November 1868, Thomas Moulsdale headed out for an afternoon of shooting. He was by no means the best marksman in the world and usually just took pot shots at small birds. After a few hours of amateur hunting the estate agent returned to his house at 6 Fountain Street, Tranmere, to relax away the rest of the day. He chatted with his mother-in-law, Mary Pickup, and told her about his shooting success.

'You should fire them off outside,' said the middle-aged woman, referring to the leftover shots. 'With so many vagrants around the workhouse it would be well to show that we have firearms in the house.'

The feared former workhouse overlooks No. 6 Fountain Street.

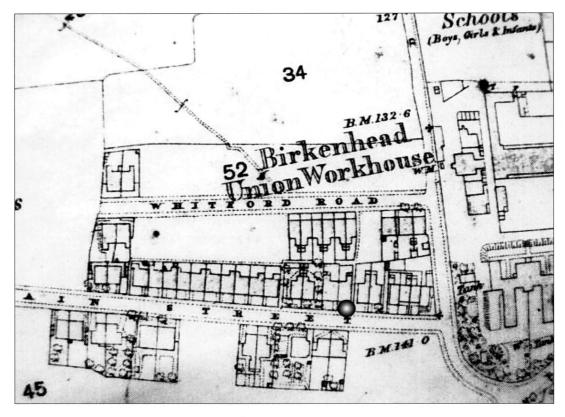

A map of Fountain Street, Tranmere.

'Good point,' replied Thomas, and he took his two guns out into the front garden. Two ear-splitting cracks sliced through the air as the remaining cartridges were sent high into the sky.

'You're a nuisance to the neighbourhood!' bawled Edward Callister, almost spitting his words out, 'a scamp and a nuisance!' He lived next door and was most annoyed at the anti-social behaviour. The two men had never been the best of friends and there had always been tension whenever they met.

'Me? You are the nuisance!' Thomas retorted as he slammed the door behind him.

Nothing more was said until just over a week later, when Thomas was heading out to attend a local political meeting. Edward was in his garden standing at the gate. He clocked him.

'What did you mean the other night by calling me a nuisance?' demanded Mr Callister.

Mr Mounsdale didn't answer but hurried off back into his hallway. On his return he was brandishing a formidable cudgel.

'What did you mean?' repeated Mr Callister.

'If you come round here I'll show you what I mean,' scoffed Thomas sarcastically. 'Do you mean to insult me?'

'Yes!' replied Mr Callister, 'not only to insult you but to assault you too!' He made a rush and landed a hard smack across the face and got Thomas into a headlock. After a brutal beating he launched the agent against some iron railings over the road, sending him into a state of battered bewilderment.

An action for damages was brought by Thomas Mounsdale the following month and he demanded £25 in compensation. The facts of the matter were deposed to a magistrate while eyewitness accounts from Mrs Pickup, Thomas' brother and a friend by the name of Mr Porter was read out. Dr Bowen stated that he had treated the plaintiff after the incident and found that Thomas had been fortunate enough not to suffer from any broken bones, but had sustained severe bruising.

His Honour thought that the initial provocation nine days earlier on the 7th could not be urged in mitigation of damage in an assault of this nature. He ruled in favour of Mr Mounsdale, forcing Edward Callsiter to pay £5 medical fees and £1 1s court costs.

A WIFE'S TALE

On 20 November 1868 Magistrates Ravenscroft and Bryans took their seats in the official chamber of the Abbey Street Court. Giving evidence that afternoon was Mrs Gibb. She was the wife of an Upton surgeon; a professional fellow who one would expect to be a respectable and decent citizen, but in reality he was nothing more than a recreant who treated his own spouse like a piece of filth.

The doctor stood cowardly before the JPs. He had been summoned before them charged with assaulting his wife several weeks previously and justice was going to be done.

A decorous Mrs Gibb took to the stand and began giving evidence against her educated brute of a husband. The magistrates heard how, on 26 October, the doctor had returned to the family home at approximately half-past two. He had been out visiting patients and had returned rather riled for some reason or other. Likewise Mrs Gibb was not in the best of moods herself. She had been having some trouble with one of the servants and wished to draw her husband's attention to the matter. Instead of listening to her qualms, he spoke sharply to her, swore angrily, and struck her across the face. Her mouth and nose began to bleed, causing fright to a young girl-servant who ran out screaming for help. Things however calmed down, for a while at least. Only hours later though Mrs Gibb was dotingly nursing their baby in a rocking chair when the doctor's disposition once again turned sour. He kicked her and again prescribed a thump across the face, sending her hurtling to the floor. The strength of the strike knocked her out and on coming to she found her husband tenderly wiping the blood from her forehead and caring for the baby.

'I'll go and get some lotion from the surgery,' said the physician, his heart seemingly beating with some compassion again. 'No, thank you,' she replied with a cold stare, 'I'd rather see Mr Inman.' Mr Inman was a local Justice of the Peace and he would certainly have something to say about the domestic abuse. Gibb knew that if the law ever found out about the maltreatment his reputation would be ruined and his practice would suffer terribly.

The coward physically prevented the woman from even leaving the house for the remainder of the day.

Come morning Mrs Gibb packed up some things and left the house to move in with her mother. She had well and truly had enough and would not be going back.

On finishing work the surgeon returned to a wifeless residence, with only his staff for company. He paid an unwanted and rather vocal visit to his mother-in-law's house in an attempt to get his partner back, but he wasn't even admitted entry.

Cross-examined, Mrs Gibb said that she had left three or four times since making the mistake of getting married; each time on account of her husband's violence. 'I cannot remember how many times he has beaten me. It is so often,' she sobbed, 'always with his fists and with kicks.' Mrs Gibb sighed that she had only returned to him in the past because she had no other place to go. The court heard how a deed of separation had since been drawn up on the woman's request. This would entitle Mrs Gibb to be free of her husband, and also entitle her to a guinea a week in maintenance.

'I won't be paying her a guinea a week to go hopping about with,' the doctor scoffed. Whilst seated he revealed some peculiar items from his breast pocket. A photograph of an unnamed gentleman and a few small various items that looked quite suitable for presents were flashed with a sinister grin. Dr Gibb held them in a taunting manner, conveying the impression to the magistrates that there were more problems with the marriage than they were privy to.

'This case is a very bad one and I am sorry to see it brought into court,' remarked Mr Ravenscroft. Mr Bryans nodded in agreement. '£5 and costs I think Mr Gibb,' announced the magistrate, 'and to bind you over sureties of £100 from yourself and two others at £50, to keep the peace towards your wife for six months.'

Mrs Gibb was delighted. She had won this round and looked optimistically forward to fighting her husband in the divorce courts.

THE BADGER BAITERS

Constable William Bennett was in plain clothes. He strolled casually towards the door of a public house at 24 Oliver Street, Birkenhead and headed in. Posing as a regular drinker Bennett paid a shilling for a ticket and ascended the series of steps to an upstairs room. His nostrils were quickly overwhelmed by a most fetid stench that seemed to overpower his entire senses. Along with the awful smell fierce yelps and growls echoed about the small and overcrowded apartment. A box in the corner, about 5ft or 6ft in length, housed a furry grey and white badger. It had been housed there for almost three years and ran around in a panic as if it knew what cruel activities lay in wait. In the centre of the room, amongst beer-swigging onlookers, sat a wire cage and, after several moments, Constable Bennett witnessed a number of rats being poured into it. They fell in with a squeal, scurrying about and nervously sniffing the walls in anxious examination.

A short time later the policeman saw a large teeth-ridden canine being led into the room. It was under the charge of a rough looking chap by the name of Thomas Gill, an unkempt blood sport fan. The rowdy crowd looked on in anticipation as Mr Gill unleashed his beast into the central cage. The animal snarled its way about the pit, tearing the rats to shreds in a carnival of carnage. Drunken drinkers sat around laughing and cheering in merriment as they peered in from overlooking benches. Rat killing seemed to be a popular pastime.

Constable Bennett was quietly making a mental record of the evening's events but his concentration was disrupted when he saw that the dog was passionately off to the corner box. As if the killing of rats wasn't enough, the animal hurried in on all fours and seized the hissing badger by the neck. The scene was nothing short of torture in the cruellest of forms. It wasn't long before the evening's entertainment got a little too heated for landlord Thomas Lawson. He became concerned that the poor badger may well die and was forced to grab the dog's tail and prise the terrified prey free with a wooden ladle. Three times the mutt was allowed to attack and three times the badger was throttled by its sharp teeth and flung about the box in a fury. The

Oliver Street, the scene of the badger baiting incident.

menacing dog was bleeding at the mouth but whether the blood was its own or the badgers could not be told, such was its vehemence.

Constable Bennett had seen enough and his colleagues were soon on the scene to offer assistance in rounding up the rapscallions and question them about their inhumane deeds.

Mr Preston held a hearing into the case soon after, on Bonfire Night 1868. The keeper of the public house, Thomas Lawson, was summoned for permitting a room in his property to be used for the purpose of badger baiting. This offence carried a maximum penalty of £5 if convicted. Also charged were no fewer that fifteen separate individuals for aiding and abetting the offence: Thomas Gill, Edward Okell, John Griffiths, Robert Nutsall, Walter Slowman, Alexander Robertson, Joseph Scott, Joseph Harvey, James McDonald,

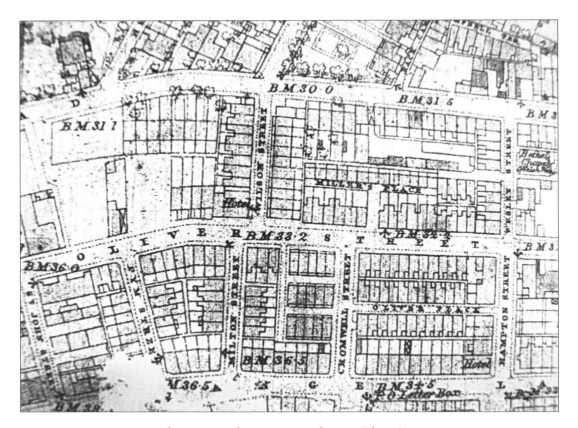

A late nineteenth-century map showing Oliver Street.

William Hall, Charles Davison, Samuel Kendrick, Edward Whitfield, George Herbert and Thomas Herbert.

PC Bennett deposed to his dealings at the pub on the night in question and testified that in his view the prisoners were indeed guilty of the offences hanging over them.

Police Inspector Gunning attested to playing a part in the operation of 24 October and recalled what he had seen. He said that there was a badger in a box with a hole in it; the badger being at the far end towards the wall. There was a rat pit in the middle of the room with branches strewn about it and cages of both live and dead rats dotted about the apartment.

The defendant, Thomas Gill, admitted that he had taken his dog to the pub with the intention of killing rats, but he swore blind that it was by total accident that the canine got into the badger box.

John Griffiths spoke next. He related how he had seen Gill's dog make an escape and head towards the box, jumping towards the badger. John remembered that the dog was swiftly removed by his fellow defendant after a few moments of hectic struggle. 'I went to the house with a gentleman who had a dog matched against another gentleman's dog to kill a certain number of rats in a certain time. I have never been to such a place before and would never care to go again!' The court tried hard to control their amusement at the man's attempt at apparent naivety, but couldn't quite manage it.

Thomas Herbert, a young, respectably dressed man, told the magistrate that he had gone to Mr Lawson's establishment on the night in question to watch what he called a 'ratting match'. For a shilling people could go up and bet on such matches in a happy and relaxed atmosphere. To him the sport was no different to darts or billiards. He corroborated with Mr Griffiths' account that Gill's dog had killed some rats then broke free of human control and went for the badger of its own animalistic accord.

Mr Preston was nearing a judgement. From the evidence it seemed perfectly clear to him that the defendant Lawson had a room in his house fitted up partly for killing rats and in the corner of the room was a box in which there was a badger. The badger had been drawn out by the dog and the defendant had permitted the act to occur. 'I'm fond as any person of any legitimate sport, but here is a cruel practice, the badger being kept in a box for three years and constantly being drawn out by dogs.' He was so revolted with the goings on that he fined Lawson the full £5 plus costs. The other accused men were each fined a shilling plus costs, with the hope that Thomas Gill would be more weary of entering such wretched places with his red-blooded canine in the future.

REGULAR JOLIFICATION

At the County Hall in Birkenhead on 13 September 1877, eleven young men were tried on a charge that would not be out of place in today's binge-drinking twenty-first century.

Superintendent Egerton told a gaggle of scholarly magistrates that on the previous Monday he had received a report of a theft from the Agricultural Show Grounds at Bidston. Barrels of beer, three in total, the property of Thomas Prescott, had been nicked. Six constables were sent to investigate the missing tipple and it was not long before they located a group of men sitting around one of the barrels enjoying its content. The two other stolen containers were nearby. When approached, the miscellany of males gasped and swore in shock at being rumbled by the Old Bill, and they staggered about in a web of directions in solo bids to escape. Alas the demon drink was too much to handle, and they each fell about in drunken tumbles to meet the long arm of the law.

Superintendent Egerton related that with the assistance of two Birkenhead constables his men were able to round up all the hazy-eyed miscreants and take them into custody. The commanding officer had been informed on the same day that a picnic had taken place earlier that afternoon, and that some members of that get-together had resorted to what he described as 'regular jollification'. Basically, they got drunk.

The accused were James Totty and John Williams, a pair of Seacombe shipwrights; Joseph Fisher and William Bennett, labourers residing at the Dock Cottages; Thomas and Joseph Parker, shipwrights of Claughton Village; Robert Williams, a rigger; sailors Anthony Malloy and Hugh Simpson; labourer Isaac Jones; and David Penington, an engine driver, all denied the charges laid against them. Most of them even had the gall to deny that they were even drunk, stating that they were merely wandering around the neighbourhood and were politely invited to have a little drink on the grass.

Unsurprisingly, each boozer was fined 5s and costs for their part in the theft and public intoxication.

CHRISTMAS CHEER

The Christmas Eve of 1891 should have been a happy and joyous occasion, a time for good will to all men and smiles all around. For one disgruntled PC, however, the festive cheer failed to yield any yuletide merriment of any sort.

Shortly before midnight on that dark winter's night, one Neptune Street front door bore the brunt of several hard taps. The owner of No. 17, Peter Atherton, heaved himself out of his chair and went to answer. On turning the latch Mr Atherton was met with a chorus of high-pitched, baby-faced carollers huddled outside. The picture-postcard scene should have been a perfect catalyst for happiness, but the children were not so angelic. They were in fact being quite noisy and causing a racket in the street. Peter didn't mind. The waterman had had a calming glass of sherry and knew the kids reasonably well; some being his very own nephews. To him the lads were just enjoying themselves as the thrill of Christmas grew ever nearer and excitement got the better of them.

PC Jones from over the road took a different view. He had been in the parlour having a drink with his fellow police officer brother when the disturbance outside gave him cause for concern. Biting his lip, the riled constable went to his doorstep and told the boys to shut up and go home. His tone was particularly harsh, especially for the time of year, and the young boys became a bit upset. Mr Atherton was furious. He ushered the children into his house as he wished to have a few strong words with his neighbour out of their earshot. He shouted across the street and began to vent, in no uncertain terms, his anger and disgust at the officer's conduct. For an hour and a half the two men argued, with the constable bounding over to Mr Atherton's doorstep, the two men squaring up nose to nose. PC Jones was behaving like a man gone mad. 'I am the boss of the street!' he barked, as the altercation grew heated. Neighbours looked on in disbelief as Jones pulled Mr Atherton from his hallway out into the street, ripping his vest in the process. Peter was accused of drunkenness, but on calling on his watching neighbours they could see that he was in fact quite sober. Nevertheless the man was arrested

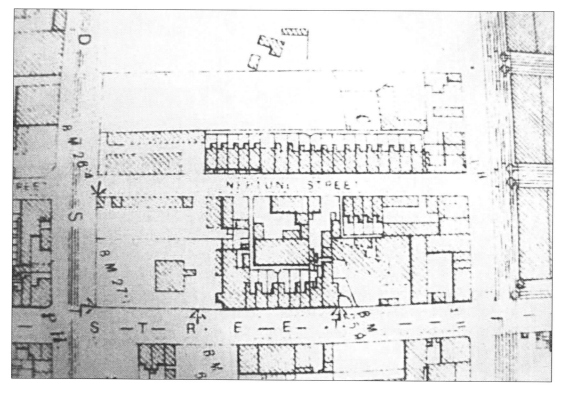

Neptune Street, c. 1900.

on a charge of being drunk and disorderly and sent to Mr Preston's court the subsequent Tuesday.

Mr Moore for the defence questioned Constable Jones over his recollections of the night's events. He had to show the court that it was the bobby who had behaved improperly and that the blame rested solely with him.

'Were these little boys not singing?'

'They were singing and shouting.'

'I see. Were you on duty?'

'I am always on duty.'

'Were you in uniform?'

Constable Jones shook his head. 'I had a cardigan jacket on.'

'Is it true that your brother tried to get you in and said that you were acting very improperly?'

'No.'

Mr Moore probed further. 'Did the neighbours say that you were acting improperly?'

'Yes, some of them did, but I knew I was not,' smiled the constable arrogantly.

'Were you drunk?'

'No.'

'Are you married?'

'No.'

'Oh that is it. I won't ask any more questions,' the solicitor shrugged, feeling as if he was getting nowhere. He took his seat amidst a few chuckles from the court.

Mr Preston listened to Jones' own versions of events, followed by Atherton's and then several witness accounts. Judging from the evidence, the magistrate believed that Mr Atherton had perhaps had one glass too many on the night in question, but he was certainly not drunk, more excitable if anything. The reports seemed to suggest to him that Constable Jones was in a similar state of slight inebriation, but was more subject to annoyance in drink. In regards to the night-time row, the spark seemed to have been set off by the actions of the officer rather than those of the defendant.

The now industrial view of Neptune Street.

'If the complainant had behaved in a judicious manner with tact and judgement, there would have been no row whatsoever. As it was he seemed to have behaved in with a roughness totally inexcusable.' The magistrate added that members of the public should be treated with respect by the police and Mr Atherton had been treated rather roughly to say the least. This was unacceptable.

The summons was dismissed with Constable Jones given a good telling off for his disreputable behaviour.

HAVOC ON THE HILL

The Saturday evening of 2 February 1884 saw Mrs Ann Webster sail back to her home in Warrington Street on the 11.15 p.m. ferry from Liverpool. She was accompanied by Mrs Marion Steel, a close friend, and the two of them disembarked arm-in-arm at Woodside. They proceeded along the dimly-lit Hamilton Street, heading back to their respective homes in Tranmere. The ladies happily meandered leisurely beneath the tall street gas lamps, chatting idle gossip until coming to a stop before a most forbidding sight. The mountain-like road that is Argyle Street South lay ahead of them, and it was with a heavy sigh that they began their nocturnal trek to the top. Mrs Steel was carrying an umbrella and it became the perfect aid in helping her ascent. During the steep climb Mrs Webster suddenly became aware that a man, one who had been on the ferry, was walking the same route ever so slightly behind them. Nothing wrong with that, Marion assumed, perhaps he lived locally. For a few moments her fear subsided.

On nearing the summit the suspicious walker grew closer. The women's hearts began to pound like jackhammers and they took a tighter hold of each other's arms in panic. The roads were unusually quiet and the walkers felt most alone and vulnerable. Only yards from the zenith of the rise, the breathless Mrs Webster was grabbed from behind and she felt a pair of heavy hands heave down on her delicate shoulders. She let out a wild scream, attracting the attention of passer-by Thomas Shaw. The startled auctioneer was walking along Whetstone Lane, but on hearing the cries ran to the hill to see an hysterical Mrs Steel whacking a man over the head with her umbrella. 'Police! Police!' screamed Mrs Webster, as the stranger maintained his hold on her back. 'Police! Please!' she pleaded.

Her attacker relinquished his grip but did not run away as the women and Mr Shaw expected. Strangely he waited for the authorities.

Inspector Astbury was soon on the scene and apprehended the man, who revealed himself to be James McCormick of 19 Star Street. At the bridewell James denied the charge of assaulting the woman, stating that it was all an innocent misunderstanding. He said that he had been walking up Argyle

The summit of Argyle Street South in 2009.

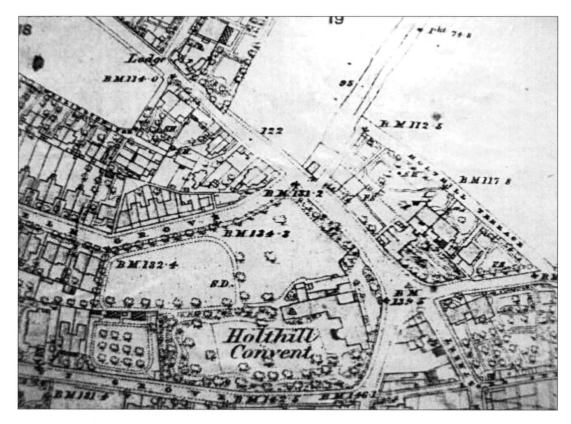

The summit of Argyle Street South, as shown in 1875.

Street South behind the ladies and that they were walking very slowly. As he neared them, walking at his normal, brisk pace, he tripped on a stone and fell onto Mrs Webster. If he hadn't grabbed hold of her back he would have fallen to the ground.

'If it was an accident then why did she scream?' asked the inspector.

Mr McCormick couldn't answer, but reminded the officer of the fact that he never attempted to escape and now offered his full apologies over the incident. Inspector Astbury didn't know what to think. It was certainly possible that the man was telling the truth and that it had indeed all been a simple mistake.

Magistrate Preston however did not share such legal hesitancy. Two days later he sentenced James McCormick to one months' imprisonment with hard labour, believing his so-called stumble to be a load of guilty codswallop.

'A BRUISED REED SHALL HE NOT BREAK'

Henry Morris was thirty-two years of age and a single dad. His wife Jane had passed away three years previously and now he was left to bring up a five-year-old son and lodge with his brother in Wallasey. Henry made his living by working at the Phospho Guano Co. in Havelock Street, unloading materials from the docks to be used in the vitriol works. The job was very stressful. Henry was responsible for a handful of men and it was a position he struggled to cope with. Drink helped him deal with the pressure but this had ultimately driven him to become an alcoholic and somewhat deranged. Mr Morris had not long been released from the insanity ward of the Birkenhead Hospital after spending a month under medical observation, when doctors considered him ready and able to return to work. Slowly but surely Henry was back at the Guano Works earning a crust for himself and his young son. Yet things were not going so well. He was still an addict and could often be found having a sly drink in the workplace. Bosses at the company could no longer tolerate his behaviour and delegated a number of Mr Morris' duties to another, more dependable, employee. He did not take the news well.

On Sunday 3 August 1884 he paid a visit to the Baptist Chapel in Falkland Road to pray at a service conducted by the Revd Logan. He was a man in truly desperate times and he asked to speak to the reverend in private. This hadn't been the first time Henry had called upon the minister for divine intervention, but as of yet God had remained impassive. During the conversation, the Revd Logan could not help but be reminded of two lines of scripture which he thought to be particularly relevant to Henry's situation.

'A bruised reed shall he not break', said the reverend, 'Jesus Christ the same yesterday, and today, and forever.'

He reminded Morris of the boundless love of the Saviour and as a gesture of faith would make those two passages the central theme of next week's service. Logan sincerely hoped Henry would be there. The labourer gave a half-hearted smile of appreciation and with an outstretched hand bid the minister goodbye.

Palermo Close is now all that remains of Henry Morris' former residence.

In reality the talk hadn't helped at all. His self-esteem had never been so low and Henry's life seemed to have lost any real purpose. Existence had never been this dire since the death of his wife, and his only real comfort was the fact that at least Jane didn't have to suffer any longer. Perhaps death was for the best.

On 9 August 1884, the residents of Palermo Street awoke to some disturbing gossip regarding the unearthly circumstances of their depressed neighbour. The details of Mr Morris' demise leaked out into the local community, bringing many who heard it to tears.

The weapon was a common pocket knife, not known for its sharpness. Indeed, Henry's was quite a dull blade and only sharp at the tip. With the knife he had slashed his face down each cheek and again down the centre of his nose. There were wounds on the chest suggesting an effort to pierce the heart, but to no avail. The tragedy had come to its miserable conclusion

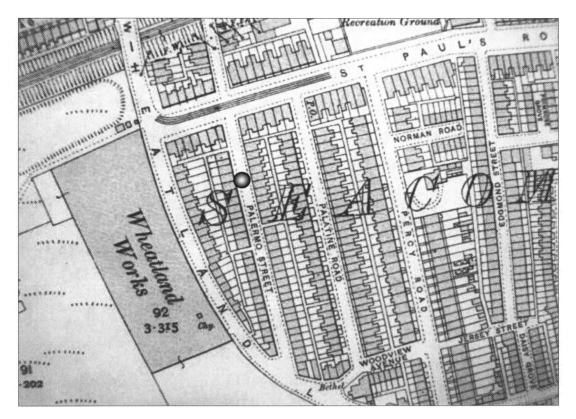

Palermo Street in Wallasey, shown on a map from the early 1900s.

when Henry turned the blade to his throat, hacking away at the neck flesh. The full horror of the act was witnessed by the man's brother. He had rushed into his bedroom upon hearing unsettling sobs and arrived just in time to witness Henry's veins peel out into the open air. The sibling ran to seek help from neighbourhood policeman, Constable Woodrow. Dr Blake was also sought, but Mr Morris died shortly afterwards. Death was due to suicide whilst temporarily insane.

The good Revd Logan kept to his word and delivered his pre-planned service the following week. At its close the minister remarked that the dear friend for whom the service was intended was no longer with them, but was where God only knew. The heart-felt nature of the address was particularly poignant and had a most sombre affect on all those present. It was said that Henry Morris himself would have been just as moved had he been able to cope with life for just one week longer.

INDEX